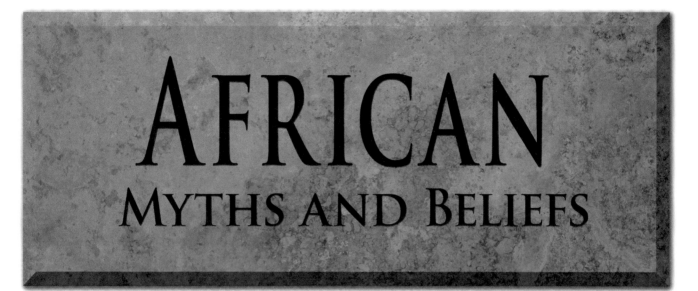

AFRICAN
MYTHS AND BELIEFS

AFRICAN
MYTHS AND BELIEFS

Tony Allan, Fergus Fleming, and Charles Phillips

ROSEN
PUBLISHING®

New York

This edition published in 2012 by:

The Rosen Publishing Group, Inc.
29 East 21st Street
New York, NY 10010

Library of Congress Cataloging-in Publication Data

Allan, Tony, 1946–
African myths and beliefs/Tony Allan, Fergus Fleming, Charles Phillips.
    p. cm.—(World mythologies)
Includes bibliographical references (p.   ) and index.
ISBN 978-1-4488-5989-4 (library binding)
1. Mythology, African. 2. Africa, Sub-Saharan—Religion. I. Fleming, Fergus, 1959– II. Phillips, Charles. III. Title.
BL2462.5.A55 2012
299.6—dc23

2011037147

Manufactured in the United States of America

CPSIA Compliance Information: Batch #W12YA: For further information, contact Rosen Publishing, New York, New York, at 1-800-237-9932.

Series copyright © 1999 Time-Life Books
Text copyright © 1999 Duncan Baird Publishers
Design and artwork copyright © 1999 Duncan Baird Publishers

Photo Credits:
The publisher would like to thank the following people, museums and photographic libraries for permission to reproduce their material. Every care has been taken to trace copyright holders. However, if we have omitted anyone we apologize and will, if informed, make corrections in any future edition.

t = top, c = center, b = bottom, l = left, r = right

Anthony Bannister Photo Library = ABPL
Bridgeman Art Library, London/New York = BAL
British Museum, London = BM
Christie's Images, London = Christie's

John Bigelow Taylor, New York = JBT
Robert Harding Picture Library = RHPL
Werner Forman Archive, London = WFA

Cover WFA; **title page** Museum fur Volkerkunde, Berlin/WFA; **contents page** WFA; **page 6** Jon Gardey/RHPL; **7** Christie's;
8 National Museum of Tanzania/WFA; **9** Chris Caldicott; **10–11** Tom Ang/RHPL; **12** Georg Gerster/Network Photographers;
14 Christie's; **15** Chris Caldicott/Royal Geographical Society; **16** BM/BAL; **17** The Sainsbury Centre for Visual Arts/University of East Anglia; **18** Museum fur Volkerkunde, Berlin/WFA; **19l** BM/WFA; **19r** Associated Press, London; **20** John Chard/Tony StoneImages; **21** JBT; **22** WFA; **23** Carol Beckwith and Angela Fisher/Robert Estall Photo Library; **24tl** David Coulson/Robert Estall Photo Library; **24bl** RHPL; **24r** BAL; **24–25** Robert Aberman; **25t** Ian Tomlinson/RHPL; **25b** David Coulson/Robert Estall Photo Library; **26** Victoria Keble-Williams/Royal Geographical Society; **27** Museum fur Volkerkunde, Berlin/WFA; **28** Roger de la Harpe/ABPL; **30** BM; **31** Royal Geographical Society; **34** Museum fur Volkerkunde, Berlin/WFA; **35** Carol Beckwith/Robert Estall Photo Library; **36** WFA; **38–39** BM/WFA; **40** BM; **41** Shaen Adey/ABPL; **42** Philip Goldman Collection/WFA; **43** Bonhams/BAL; **44–45** Christie's; **46** Chris Caldicott; **47** BM; **48–49** BM; **49** Christie's; **50l** Christie's; **50c** Royal Geographical Society; **50r** National Museum of Tanzania/WFA; **51l** Peter Holmes/RHPL; **51t** RHPL; **51b** Christie's; **52** Her Majesty The Queen, via the BM; **53** Indianapolis Museum of Art, Gift of Mr and Mrs Harrison Eiteljorg; **54** JBT; **55** RHPL; **56** RHPL; **57** WFA; **58** Chris Caldicott; **59** Royal Museum for Central Africa, Turveren, Belgium/BAL; **60** The Sainsbury Centre for Visual Arts/ University of East Anglia; **62** RHPL; **64** Michael Holford; **66** Christie's; **67** Christie's; **69** Horniman Museum and Gardens, London; **70** JBT; **71** WFA; **72** Museum fur Volkerkunde, Berlin/WFA; **75** UCLA Fowler Museum of Cultural History, California, photo: Denis J. Nervig; **76l** Christina Dodwell/Hutchison Picture Library; **76r** Christie's; **77t** RHPL; **77b** Pitt Rivers Museum, Oxford; **78** Musee Royal de l'Afrique Centrale, Turveren, photo: R. Asselberghs; **79** Christie's; **80–81** Walter Rawlings/RHPL; **82** Christie's; **84** Christie's; **86** BM/BAL; **87** Christie's; **90** Christie's; **91** Chris Bradley/Axiom; **92** WFA; **95** Museum of South Africa, Cape Town, South Africa; **96** Christie's; **97** David Constantine/Axiom; **99** WFA; **101** WFA; **102** JBT; **103** WFA/BM; **104–105** Musee Dapper, Paris; **107** Indiana University Art Museum, Bloomington, Indiana; **108** Horniman Museum and Gardens, London; **109** WFA; **111** Mary Jeliffe/Hutchison Picture Library; **112l** BM/Michael Holford; **112b** Bryan & Cherry Alexander; **113** Bryan & Cherry Alexander; **114t** Simon Westcott/RHPL; **114b** Andrea Booher/Tony Stone Images; **115t** Simon Westcott/RHPL; **115b** Horniman Museum and Gardens, London; **116** Museum fur Volkerkunde, Berlin/WFA; **117** Christie's; **118** Christie's; **119** BM/WFA; **120** WFA; **121** Horniman Museum and Gardens, London; **122** Entwhistle Gallery/WFA; **124** WFA; **125** Christie's; **126** Sybil Sassoon/Royal Geographical Society; **127** BM; **129** AISA, Barcelona; **130** BM; **131** BM; **132** Nik Wheeler/RHPL; **133** BM; **134** Horniman Museum and Gardens, London; **135** Redferns; **136** WFA; **137** Ronald Grant Archive, London.

Contents

Yoruba Sango carving of a horse, a
woman and child, and various followers,
representing the attributes of wealth,
fertility, and power.

CRADLE OF HUMANKIND

One of the many things that struck nineteenth-century imperialists about Africa was its size: the continent was three times the area of Europe and Scandinavia combined; the Sahara Desert alone was almost the size of the United States and contained a single rock plateau almost as large as France; the Niger delta covered a massive 14,016 square miles (36,000 km^2)—and the Niger was by no means Africa's greatest river. Within this vastness lay almost every kind of topography known to humankind. The Sahara and Kalahari deserts to the north and south respectively were among the Earth's most uninhabitable zones, their eroded landscapes yielding reluctantly to a more hospitable fringe of savannah. In direct contrast, West and Central Africa were home to sultry, equatorial rainforests. Yet, if one followed the equator to the east one discovered snow-capped mountains and gentle, rolling farmlands. Southern Africa, meanwhile, comprised mile upon mile of high-altitude veldt whose hot, dry days and freezing evenings mellowed as a traveler dropped south into the Mediterranean climate of the Cape or the humidity of Natal.

The continent was not particularly human-friendly: its rainforests bred devastating viruses; parasites were rife; and vitamin deficiency was endemic. River-blindness, dengue fever, bilharzia, malaria, and a host of other maladies were commonplace. Swaths of the continent were infested by the tsetse fly whose bite was fatal to humans, cattle, and horses alike. Yet its inhabitants flourished, adopting lifestyles suited to their differing environments.

Culturally, Africa was as varied as its landscape. Its people ranged from the Stone Age to the urbane. Their languages were myriad and their history was intense: empires the size of Rome had come and gone in Africa while Europe struggled through its Middle Ages. And their myths were multitudinous. They drew spiritual inspiration from their surroundings: the teeming wildlife, a mountain, a river, or even the humble yam. They worshipped their own deities as well as the imported gods of Islam and Christianity. Underlying all, however, was a sense of timelessness. Africa was the birthplace of humankind and its lore, passed down the generations by word of mouth, reflected humanity's first musings on the universe. In that respect it was bigger than the colonialists could ever have imagined.

Opposite: The African environment varied massively and the human cultures with it, from desert-living hunter-gatherers to savannah pastoralists, and from fishermen and traders on the coast to inland farmers. For many semi-nomadic peoples cattle, seen here in Niger, were central to life.

Left: The items of beaded jewelry that adorn this carved wooden figure are magical objects intended to enhance its power. Songye prestige bowl, Congo, late 19th or early 20th century.

7

Africa and Its Peoples

For hundreds of thousands of years what was to become the Sahara Desert was an expanse of mountain-dotted savanna that provided rich pickings for humans and animals alike. But millennia of rainfall washed nutrients from the soil and turned it a sullen red color. With the population growing and the land beginning to dry out, its inhabitants drifted south.

The Early Hunter-gatherers

Africa's first human inhabitants were principally hunters who spread over the continent and reached its southern tip millions of years ago. Peoples such as the Khoi, the San, and the Kung are considered the survivors of this once wide-spread population. They foraged through the landscape for plants and grubs, and used arrows to bring down animals such as gazelle, eland, and quagga—a now-extinct relative of the zebra.

Practicing a largely non-material culture, the foragers' distinctive language of clicks and rasps carried a rich lore of stories and knowledge of the natural world; they also sang and played music. Rock outcrops decorated with their colorful images of daily life existed from the earliest times. Moving in small family groups from camp to camp—a clump of trees, perhaps, or a cave—the early Africans had little social structure save the sexual division of labor: hunting was a male prerogative, foraging a job for females. The former was the more skilled and prestigious occupation; the latter, however, was the most productive—although game was plentiful its supply was erratic, depending largely on seasonal migrations; roots and fruits, on the other hand, were always available to those who knew where to look. The allocation of gender roles was duly reflected in their mythology—and later in those of other African societies—with divinely attributed gifts or events having male or female relevance.

Today's representatives of humankind's oldest lifestyle, the Khoi and their ilk were even then behind the times: the benefits of settled agriculture

Stone Age rock art of a shamanistic dance known as a *simbo*, which causes a state of trance in the participant. The image of the antelope head suggests the early potency of animal symbols.

The First Humans

The African continent witnessed the dawn of humankind. Archaeologists have found fossil evidence to suggest that Africa saw the emergence not only of the first hominids— our most distant ancestors to walk on two legs—but also the first recognizable human, **Homo habilis.**

Two million years ago, Olduvai Gorge, Tanzania, was a lake surrounded by lush vegetation, but gradually it silted up and expanded. Over the millennia the waters drained down a river that carved a massive gorge through the sediment. In the late 1920s, British archaeologists Louis and Mary Leakey started to examine the fossils protruding from the sides of the gorge.

For thirty years the Leakeys uncovered many man-made artifacts, but no traces of people. Then, in 1959, Mary found the 1.75-million-year-old skull of a hominid and they called the species *Zinjanthropus*. The next year Louis unearthed the oldest known skull of *Homo habilis*, or "handy man."

The 49 in^3 (800 cm^3) brain of *Homo habilis* was unique for its time. It permitted tool-making abilities, the prime characteristic that distinguished humans from their hominid predecessors. Sifting through the gorge, the Leakeys also found a multitude of more recent implements that were produced by the successor to *Homo habilis*, *Homo erectus*.

Meanwhile, other regions of Africa were yielding their secrets. In 1974 anthropologist Donald Johanson unearthed a skeleton in Ethiopia that was 3.25 million years old. It belonged to a female hominid whom he named Lucy. And in

The exposed sides of Olduvai Gorge have yielded some of the oldest remains of humankind's ancestors.

December 1998 archaeologists unearthed hominid remains of a similar age in South Africa, thus proving that humankind's ancestors were not restricted to Africa's East Coast but roamed elsewhere on the continent too.

had been known in the Middle East since approximately 9000 BCE. But such was Africa's bounty that they had no need to farm. There were more than enough roots and berries to meet their demands—indeed, some studies suggest that hunter-gatherers had a far greater variety of food than agriculturally dependent settled peoples. Different types of fish abounded in most freshwater streams and lakes, and huge herds of animals migrated across the southern veldt. As late as the nineteenth century Europeans reported the movement of gazelle in waves that reached miles to the horizon. Given, too, the relative smallness of their population compared to the size of their territory, they had little incentive to change.

People of the Rainforest

Another branch of hunter-gatherers, meanwhile, had settled in the rainforests of equatorial Africa. Diminutive pygmy peoples, such as the Mbuti and Twa, they were physically unique, being rarely more than 3.9 feet (1.2 m) tall.

The pygmies derived the same diversity of foodstuffs from their surroundings as did their cousins farther south, and their lifestyle was equally successful—if not more so. When farming finally reached southern Africa, bushmen such as the Kung were to become marginalized on the desert fringes. Secure in the forest depths, however, many pygmy peoples were to survive happily alongside their new neighbors.

Pastoralists

Hunter-gatherers were the oldest but by no means the only strand of African life. From 5000 BCE they were joined by pastoralists—such as today's Somali and Masai in the east and the Fulani in the west—who were devoted to the rearing and herding of livestock. These semi-nomadic peoples roamed the western and eastern savannah in small clans of inter-related families accompanied by their animals, mainly cattle. The pattern of their lives was dictated by the availability of water and pasture. During the wet season—typically between April and September, when monsoon rains swept in from the Indian Ocean—they exploited the new growth of marginal areas. In the dry season they moved to more dependable zones, such as the mountains, where cooler, damper conditions prevailed. Within these broad extremes, however, they could be affected by any number of local variations: wells might fail; the rains might be late and the vegetation poor; or the rains might be prolonged and disease prevalent— wet conditions encouraged the tsetse fly, fatal to humans and cattle alike. In these cases their only option was to move quickly to better ground—the existence of which was by no means certain.

In this unsettled world, material possessions were few—the faster a family could strike camp the sooner it could find richer pastures. For certainties they depended upon their heritage—most

The Wealth of Herds

For pastoralists, such as the Somali, the Pokot, the Fulani, the Masai, and the Dinka, the cow was almighty. It provided everything a person could need—meat and milk for food, leather for clothes, and horn and bone for implements.

A cow's slaughter was not contemplated lightly, however, for in times of uncertainty it was a walking larder. The Fulani often lived off nothing but milk products when other supplies ran short. The Masai went one step further, drawing cattle blood to provide liquid sustenance. In the absence of coins, cows were the measure of wealth, and remained so among pastoralists even when a currency of cowrie shells and metal bars had become commonplace in the eighteenth century.

If a man lost his cows, he was to all intents and purposes dead. This was well demonstrated in the rinderpest epidemic that hit West Africa in 1897. Whole herds were annihilated and their Fulani owners shaved their heads, discarded their clothes, and wandered naked through the bush eating dust. They had lost their livestock, their place in society, and their reason for living.

The inhabitants of the Sahel and savanna areas depended on cattle for their livelihood. A herder near Baragoi, Kenya.

families could trace their bloodline to a single, named male ancestor—and, above all, their cattle, whose pedigree was of equal importance.

The lives of men and women alike were inextricably linked to their herds. At birth, every male child was granted a small number of cows that would form the nucleus of a herd he was destined to care for in later years. Marriage was marked by a gift of cows and adulthood was concerned with the raising of calves that would eventually become the marriage payments for the couple's offspring. And when all their children had married, and their cattle had passed to the next generation, the parents became unnecessary. To the Fulani, their elders were little better than living ghosts. Lacking cattle, they lacked social meaning and were forced to eke out their lives on the outskirts of settlements.

Disease was the scourge of pastoral society, but was usually avoidable: people knew from experience how to avoid the tsetse fly. Less predictable was human depredation. The warlike Somali thought nothing of stealing cattle from one another and attacking their neighbors. And from the late eighteenth century onwards the Fulani, fired with Islamic religious zeal, spread over a territory large enough to be classified as an empire. Generally, however, aggressive politics did not feature in pastoral life; most people were too preoccupied with the struggle against nature.

11

Settled Agriculturalists

By the very nature of their existence, pastoralists moved on, wandering in the rain-fed savannas between the desert and the forests, and in East Africa they moved down the drier plateaus and reached the jungles of Central Africa. But by about 3000 BCE agriculture had been invented in sub-Saharan Africa (from where people are thought to have moved north along the Nile, bringing with them typically African crops that then were supplemented with the millet first grown in the Middle East). Fertile equatorial zones along the Niger River and around Lake Chad became home to settled, year-round farming communities. The Niger River basin in particular nurtured a number of civilizations, including the Yoruba complex along the lower half and the Sahelian Djenne group above the central delta. Pastoralists who ventured thus far were either repulsed or were absorbed into the new way of life.

Scattered across the waist of sub-Saharan Africa, agricultural communities kept a limited amount of livestock but concentrated mostly on raising the staples best suited to their region. Two root crops, yams and cassava, were widespread. In the mid-east these were supplemented by bananas and groundnuts. Later, in the nineteenth century, the humid climate of West Africa provided perfect conditions for rice paddies; the more temperate eastern countries adapted readily to wheat cultivation. Their crops influenced their mythologies: the Ibo of Nigeria spoke of yams; the Liberian Kpelle of rice; and the Suku, in the Congo, of cassava. And again, the male-female division of labor was evident—women generally tended the crops, while men engaged in quicker, more intensive tasks that left enough free time to discuss politics and exercise their influence.

Settled life brought social changes. Family attachments were still respected: most farmers clustered in villages whose inhabitants descended from a common ancestor; groups of villages together formed a clan. Permanence, however, required a degree of government, and even the smallest settlement had some kind of political hierarchy. Just as lineage elders often controlled the usage rights of land, thus enhancing the importance of kinship ties, so social structures were often organized by age. The Ibo villagers of what is now Nigeria, for example, drew their governing bodies from three age groups, of which the junior executive was drawn from men aged between fifty-five and sixty-four. The most senior category started at eighty-four. This contrasted radically with their pastoral neighbors, the Fulani, for whom middle-aged men were considered unnecessary.

Agriculture was vastly more productive than pastoralism and cultivated areas supported larger

Right: **The map shows the principal topographical areas of Africa, revealing the mix of arid, fertile, and forested land that influenced patterns of settlement and lifestyle. The proximity of Arabia provided a trade and cultural influence in the east.**

Left: **Granaries and houses in Labbe Zanga, Mali, reflect the inter-related, organic pattern of village life.**

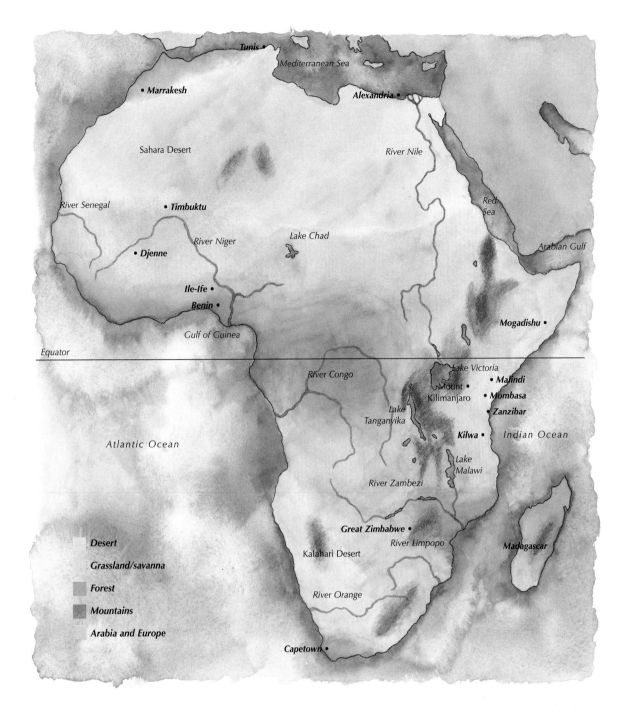

The following labels appear on the map:

Tunis

Mediterranean Sea

Marrakesh

Alexandria

Sahara Desert

River Nile

River Senegal

Red Sea

Timbuktu

Arabian Gulf

River Niger

Lake Chad

Djenne

Ile-Ife

Benin

Gulf of Guinea

Mogadishu

Equator

River Congo

Lake Victoria

Mount Kilimanjaro

Malindi

Mombasa

Zanzibar

Lake Tanganyika

Atlantic Ocean

Kilwa

Indian Ocean

Lake Malawi

River Zambezi

Great Zimbabwe

River Limpopo

Madagascar

Kalahari Desert

Desert

Grassland/savanna

Forest

Mountains

Arabia and Europe

River Orange

Capetown

populations—the basin of the lower Niger was especially congested—but it was by no means an easy alternative. It was subject to the same natural disasters of drought and disease, to which were added the human factors of warfare and slavery, both dismal products of a settled existence. Moreover, survival was now down to individual rather than collective effort. Whether a man prospered or failed was entirely the result of his own endeavor; no one else would farm his fields for him. In this new, harder society, the ethos was one of self-improvement. Material and social status could only be achieved by hard work.

Making and Trading Goods
Materialism did not feature in the cultures of either hunter-gathers or pastoralists—possessions were only

13

a hindrance to people constantly on the move. The seasonal nature of agriculture, however, combined with the surplus of food it produced, freed people to concentrate on other tasks. Cotton was grown, mines were dug, trees were felled, and small-scale manufacturing became commonplace. Most societies boasted blacksmiths, weavers, carpenters, potters, and a variety of other artisans. The Yoruba of West Africa, meanwhile, became virtually an industrial nation. To one British explorer in the 1820s their cotton goods compared in quality—if not quite in quantity—to anything emanating from his homeland. But generally, such work was an adjunct to the more serious business of food production.

A World of Plentiful Wealth

When the outside world took notice of sub-Saharan Africa it was not—with the notable exception of West African textiles—because of the goods it manufactured. Rather, it was on account of its vast natural wealth. Since the days of ancient Egypt, Africa has supplied the globe with gold, diamonds, ivory, mahogany, minerals, spices, exotic feathers, and pelts; throughout medieval Europe, precious metals were traded that had originated in Africa, thus contributing to dreams of the legendary wealth that might be had there.

The continent also offered a more ghastly trade—one rooted in antiquity, but for which there was huge, continuing demand: human slaves. Caravans made their way through

The bold red and copper or brass bowl shape of this male dancer's helmet reflect eastern influences, possibly Ethiopian. Latuka people, Sudan.

the Sahara Desert to pick whole districts clean. Many people died en route; some estimates suggest that one-third of the "human cargo" perished. Slavery became so firmly established that it entered many societies' penal codes.

While some of Africa's trade flowed overland, by far the largest proportion was conducted by sea. As a result, coastal communities emerged whose culture was a hybrid of African and foreign influences. Of these, by far the most powerful were those of East Africa, whose hegemony eventually extended from Mogadishu in the north to Mozambique in the south. The name of the island of Zanzibar is a memento of the days when it was an outpost of Persia's Zenj empire, while the word "Swahili" derives from the Arabic term "sawahali," or "of the coast."

Powers of East and West

Culturally and economically, the East African Swahili were Africa's middlemen. They exported goods from the interior to Persia, India, China, and the East Indies, receiving in return not only money but skills and artifacts from around the world. From the Arabs they acquired navigational skills, the Islamic religion, and a flowing script with which they transcribed their oral literature. Their cities were built in a distinctive Middle-Eastern style and were decorated with ceramics from Asia. They spoke a unique language that drew upon those of their trading partners. They adopted urban lifestyles and arrayed themselves in cosmopolitan fashion. "They wear fine silk and cotton garments bought. . . from the [Indian] merchants," wrote an impressed traveler in the sixteenth century CE. "Their women, too, go bravely dressed and wear jewels of fine Sofala gold, of silver in plenty, with earrings, necklaces, bangles, bracelets; and their clothing, too, is of silk."

In the west, matters were different. Here, on the aptly named Ivory, Gold, and Slave coasts, a more militaristic spirit prevailed thanks to the influence of Europe. When the first Portuguese traders arrived in West Africa in the fifteenth century, in

The Influence of Islam

Introduced to sub-Saharan Africa by Arab traders from about 800 CE, Islam became one of the continent's dominant religions and had a profound influence on African culture.

Islam was of non-African origin, but buildings such as the mosque at Diafarabe, Mali, took indigenous form.

Islam put down its deepest roots in the coastal cities of East Africa such as Mombasa and Kilwa where literacy in Arabic became reasonably widespread.

By contrast, Islam in West Africa was practiced by an elite. Rulers and their families converted, lending Islam prestige—particularly when their nations were powerful, as was gold-rich Mali in the fourteenth century.

Initially, Islam coexisted with local traditions. By the nineteenth century, however, it had taken a more aggressive form with its adherents seeking to ban other beliefs—including the newly arrived Christianity.

The new proselytizing created organized, urban-led states in previously agricultural areas. Some Fulani, for example, turned their backs on pastoral life and became civic rulers, adopting the religion that earlier West African potentates had espoused. They celebrated their newfound status in a myth that gained currency across the north of West Africa (see pages 122–123). In it, a traveling hero visits a town only to find that its water supply is threatened by a monstrous water-serpent. Slaying the beast the man becomes the town's ruler. That he is a Muslim goes unsaid.

Power aside, Islam held other attractions for Africans. As cities burgeoned in the nineteenth and twentieth centuries—ironically, as a result of Western, Christian colonization—immigrants took to Islam as a way of melting into the crowd. And then there was the fact that Islam was the only pan-African force to withstand the pressure of Europeanization. Its role as the underdog religion won it popular support.

Such sentiment was, however, possibly misplaced. Islamic states in North Africa and Arabia had operated a slave trade long before the West and continued to do so long after.

the course of their search for Indian spices, they had simply wanted gold and ivory. It was a fair enough arrangement—the Africans got the manufactured products they desired and the Europeans got the raw materials they coveted. Both sides profited—particularly the Europeans: one of the first English traders made a 1,000 percent return on his capital outlay for the trip.

The Misery of Slavery

From the sixteenth century, however, following the discovery of the West Indies and the subsequent development of plantation economies requiring cheap labor, Europeans wanted not so much gold as slaves. Local rulers were initially agreeable, always having a number of criminals or social outcasts who were excess to requirements (nineteenth-century explorers recorded many eyewitness accounts of large, annual ritual executions). Demand, however, soon outstripped supply and to maintain the influx of foreign goods on which their prestige depended, chiefs turned to warfare as the easiest means of obtaining the necessary number of slaves. Great slave-taking and slave-trading kingdoms arose, and the use of European weapons as payment created a dynamic that fueled the business still further. A Portuguese account of 1506 noted: "At the mouth of the Senegal River you find the first black peoples, and that is the beginning of the kingdom of Jolof. Its king can put 10,000 cavalry and 100,000 infantry into the field." There were many others like him along the coast in Dahomey, Oyo, and Benin.

Brass was of greater value than gold in much of West Africa, although the Ashanti peoples prized gold very highly. Human-head mask, Ghana.

When compared to the east, there was little cultural exchange. The Africans gained nothing from Europe save firearms, cheap manufactured goods—whose ownership was reserved for the privileged—and a closer acquaintance with economic ruin. Whole nations were devastated by the abstraction of their labor force, and despondent farmers began to ignore even the most basic tenets of agriculture. Why not slaughter a cow in calf? It might be your last meal as a free man.

Some African rulers protested. So did some Western governments. But when a neighboring African ruler was willing to supply slaves, and a neighboring European nation was willing to buy them, there was not much either side could do. Britain banned the slave trade in 1807 and took steps to enforce the measures, but others continued an official trade until the middle of the nineteenth century—by which time an estimated 14 million Africans had embarked for the Americas, some two million of them never to arrive.

Great Kingdoms of a Continent

Slavery aside, the combined pressures of domestic development and foreign contact occasionally bore spectacular fruit. African kingdoms and empires arose whose wealth and administrative capabilities frequently exceeded those of the states with whom they traded. As early as 800 BCE, the kingdoms to the south of Egypt in places like Ethiopia and Nubia were on equal terms with their pyramid-building neighbors. At times, indeed, Nubian pharaohs actually governed Egypt. The emperors of Ethiopia, meanwhile, boasted a lineage that descended from

Solomon. True, their family tree may have owed more to wishful thinking than genetics, but this did not prevent them from creating a state in the first century CE of which the Biblical ruler would have been proud. It was still extant in 1774 when a Scottish traveler, James Bruce, visited the area and brought back tales of a monarch who governed with impressive pomp, whose cavalry wore chain mail, and whose infantry numbered 30,000. His report was widely discounted. In 1896, however, when invading Italians were soundly defeated by Ethiopian forces, it was allowed that his stories might have some credence. And when the pride of Mussolini's army struggled to conquer Ethiopia in 1936, it was thought they were probably true.

Ethiopia was one of Africa's most tenacious sovereignties—its last emperor, Haile Selassie, the self-styled Lion of Judah, was not deposed until 1974. But there were many other, shorter-lived kingdoms whose power was just as great. From the eighth century onward the demand for gold gave enormous prestige to the ore-rich nations of West Africa whose rulers spent lavishly and ostentatiously. For two centuries, from about 1580, much of what is now the state of Nigeria was occupied by the Yoruba city-states whose bureaucracy was comparable to anything then existing in Europe. Farther west, the Fon and Ashanti confederacies were regarded with awe not only by Africans but by the Europeans who subjugated them—with considerable difficulty—in the nineteenth century. But the Yoruba were descended from the much older and more powerful Nok culture, some 2,000–3,000 years old, which in turn fragmented into city-states, the last of which was Oyo.

On the east coast, meanwhile, the Swahili produced city-ports of phenomenal wealth such as Mombasa, in modern Kenya, and Kilwa, an island off the coast of Tanzania. They exchanged ambassadors with courts throughout Asia, and their trading fleets were a marvel to behold. "The

Chieftainship

Most African rulers claimed to be empowered by divine ancestry but this did not necessarily give them absolute power.

The kingdom of Buganda, in East Africa, was in many ways typical. It enjoyed a sophisticated and centralized government. Supreme authority was vested in the king, or *kabaka*, beneath whom rested a pyramid of lesser chiefs. The kingdom was divided into ten separate counties, each with its own chief. Beneath these chiefs were subcounty chiefs—usually six in number—who controlled sections of counties. And below them in turn were further strata, the lowest of whom were the village chiefs.

Accountability flowed back up the pyramid, each chief being answerable to his immediate superior. Ultimate responsibility, however, always rested with the *kabaka*. It was he who appointed most of his underlings and who promoted, transferred, or dismissed them. The system was designed to promote efficiency but also to prevent any subordinate seizing power.

Outwardly despotic, the *kabaka*'s rule was constrained by a number of checks. He was not born to the post but was elected from the royal family by his most senior chiefs. Decision-making was dependent on a body of councilors, and if he was widely unpopular or incompetent he was often overthrown.

The *kabaka* system of kingship was echoed widely through the continent. A royal scepter and symbol of chieftainship; elephant ivory, Benin, 16th–18th century.

17

ships that sail the southern seas are like houses," recorded a fifteenth-century Chinese writer. "When their sails are spread they are like great clouds in the sky. Their rudders are several tens of feet long. A single ship carries several hundred men, and stores a year's supply of grain." Kilwa, known from about 1100 CE as the "Queen of the South," sat on a majestic bay that was large enough, according to nineteenth-century Britons, to hold half the Royal Navy. Its ruler's palace boasted the largest rooms in Africa and was equipped with luxuries such as an octagonal bath, set on a cliff-top, from which the king and his ladies could admire the last rays of light on the Indian Ocean. Mombasa, Kilwa's close rival, was almost as grand. "It is a very fair place," wrote a fifteenth-century Portuguese traveler, "with lofty stone and mortar houses, well aligned in streets. It is a place of much trade. . ." For more than three centuries, until they were sacked by Europeans in the early 1500s, Kilwa and Mombasa were peaceful, prosperous places. Few, if any, Western nations can claim such a history.

The commercial acuity of the Swahili was not confined to the coast. Farther inland it created the great empire of Monomotapa in modern-day Zimbabwe. Centered on the vast, circular structures of its capital, Great Zimbabwe, Monomotapa was the center of a massive cattle-herding economy. It was also a major gold producer, nuggets of the mineral simply lying on the ground waiting to be picked up. During Monomotapa's heyday, its influence extended over huge tracts of southern Africa, spawning smaller *zimbabwes*—the name means "house of stone"—as far distant as modern Transvaal. It collapsed in around 1834 from a combination of human and natural causes. In the 1870s, however, when Europeans stumbled upon the remains of Great Zimbabwe, it enjoyed a posthumous resurgence. Unable to believe that Africans were capable of

TIMELINE	2,500,000–0 BCE

Enormous, ancient, and populous, Africa was in all probability both the place of origin for humankind as a species and the land that people first left in order to colonize the rest of the world. Home to vast mineral wealth, various empires have risen and fallen in Africa through the centuries and hundreds of cultures have blossomed. Long in touch with the riches and innovations of the east, from the fifteenth century onward Africa became the coveted prize of ambitious European nations that were themselves seeking the exotic produce of the east. Exploration became subjugation and colonization, with the human misery of slavery causing forced emigration to the Americas on a massive scale. Today, however, Africa is redefining itself in its own, distinct way.

c.2,500,000 BCE Early Stone Age culture practiced by Australopithecines.
c.2,000,000 BCE Archaic humans, *Homo habilis*, known to have been using tools.
c.1,400,000 BCE *Homo erectus* dispersed throughout the continent.
c.100,000 BCE Modern humans, *Homo sapiens*, left Africa to colonize the world.
c.9000 BCE Wet period, which lasted several millennia, helped the grasslands, rivers, and lakes expand, with benefical effects for both animals and humans.
c.7000 BCE Various early productive economies pioneered.
c.5000 BCE Prehistoric Khoi, San, and Kung hunter-gatherers widely dispersed across the continent. Pastoralism appeared in savanna Africa, involving cattle, goats, and sheep.
c.3000 BCE Settled farming communities established in the fertile, equatorial regions. Ancient Egypt united under kingship system.
c.1000 BCE Ironmaking spread throughout Africa.
c.800 BCE Ethiopian and Nubian kingdoms rivaled the power of Egypt.

A terracotta head from the Yoruba city-state of Ile-Ife, 12th–15th century.

creating such complex buildings, they decided it could only be the land from which the Queen of Sheba brought her wealth to Israel. Droves of prospectors descended on the ruins in search of the legendary "King Solomon's Mines." They did little save destroy a valuable archaeological site. One man, however, did find some gold—nobody knows how much—and so the legend persisted.

Southern Migration

While empires rose and fell, a less monumental but equally important development was affecting sub-Saharan Africa. This was the migration of Bantu-speaking peoples from their equatorial homelands into the southern reaches of the continent. By the eleventh century one branch had settled on the South African high veldt and a century later another was pushing south along the coast of present-day Natal. In the vanguard of this latter group were the Xhosa, whose way of life by and large served as a paradigm of Bantu existence. They were farmers, whose economy and culture were inextricably linked to the cattle they tended. They rode cows, raced cows, and sacrificed cows, when occasion demanded, to their ancestors. They composed poems to them, paraded them at important festivals, and used them as a measure of wealth, particularly in the matter of marriage payments. Male children were formed into age groups whose most important step came at the age of about ten, when they were deemed fit to herd cows. Adulthood was marked, some ten years later, by a ceremony to prove that they were no longer herders but fully fledged farmers capable of owning their own cattle. The cow was a sacred totem of masculinity. Women were not even allowed to wash a milking pail. To them, instead, fell the task of growing the crops—maize, millet, sweet potatoes, beans, and peas—that were the Xhosa's dietary staples.

On the whole, life was peaceful. Although the Xhosa were divided into chiefdoms, matters were decided more by debate than dictat. Political oratory was a respected skill, and a well-developed

1 CE–1830	1831–1885	1886–PRESENT DAY

c.1 CE–500 Bantu peoples expanded southward.
1100 Kilwa and Mombasa on the Indian Ocean prospered as trading centers for East Africa and the Arabian Gulf.
1200 The empire of Monomotapa established its principal city at Great Zimbabwe.
1235 Sunjata Keita established the empire of Mali along the upper Niger.
1444–1471 Portugal established bases in West Africa, including Cape Verde and Elmina.
1505 Kilwa and Mombasa were sacked by European forces.
1580 High point of the Yoruba kingdom of Oyo began and lasted for some 200 years.
1787 Territory of Sierra Leone established for freed slaves by British abolitionists.
1804 Uthman Dan Fodio launched the first Fulani Islamic jihad in northern Nigeria.
1807 Britain abolished the trade in slaves.
1818 Shaka succeeded Chief Dingiswayo of the Zulu and intensified the *mfecane*.
1830 France conquered Algeria, Europe's first African outpost.

1833 Slavery ended in the British empire.
1834 Great Zimbabwe collapsed.
1830s Great Trek undertaken by Dutch settlers (Boers and Afrikaners) to evade British rule.
1852–1854 Boers created the republics of the Orange Free State and Transvaal.
1852–1862 Islamic empire established by al-Hajj Umar Tal, across West Africa.
1849–1873 David Livingstone undertook journeys of exploration and missionary activity.
1869 Suez Canal opened. Diamonds found in Kimberley, South Africa.
1874–1877 H.M. Stanley solved the riddle of the sources of the Nile and Congo rivers.
1876 King Leopold II of Belgium called a conference of explorers in Brussels to garner support for development of the continent.
1884 Europeans at the Congress of Berlin partitioned Africa.
1885 Gold found in Transvaal.

Armed Portuguese soldier depicted on a brass plaque from the palace of the oba of Benin, 16th century.

Nelson Mandela campaigns during multiracial elections in newly democratic South Africa.

1896 Invading Italian forces defeated in Ethiopia.
1936 Haile Selassie appealed to the League of Nations for Africa to be left alone. Fascist Italy struggled to conquer Ethiopia.
1957 Period of decolonization began throughout Africa with the independence of Ghana, a former British colony.
1959 Mary Leakey discovered the skull of hominid species *Zinjanthropus*, some 1.75 million years old.
1960 Louis Leakey discovered the skull of *Homo habilis*.
1961 Apartheid system of racial discrimination introduced in South Africa.
1974 Ethiopia's last emperor deposed.
1994 Multiracial democracy established in the Republic of South Africa.
1997 Ghana's Kofi Annan became Secretary-General of the United Nations.

19

legal system prevailed. In Xhosa law, a man was innocent until proven guilty. Punishment was commonly a fine of cattle; occasionally a gross offender was executed. If they had to fight, however, they were prepared to do so, forming themselves into spear-wielding battalions that were organized according to age group and overseen by a single leader.

Generally the call to arms came only when the land's original inhabitants, the Khoi, objected to having their grazing overrun by strangers. But in the early nineteenth century the Xhosa found themselves having to fight with increasing frequency. The reason for this was that the Xhosa's southward march had been checked by another group of migrants moving north from the Cape. These were the Boers, the white descendants of Dutch settlers who had landed at Capetown during the seventeenth century. Like the Xhosa, the Boers were, by and large, cattle farmers. Like the Xhosa they had seized their pastures from the Khoi. And like the Xhosa they saw no reason why they should not continue to expand outwards. Unlike the Xhosa, however, they possessed firearms. The clash between Boer and Xhosa took place on Great Fish River and culminated from 1835 in a series of treaties—brokered by British artillery—that drove the Xhosa steadily north.

Chameleons and Flies

Britain's involvement stemmed from its annexation of the Cape to protect the trade route to India. The Cape was its first African colony but by no means its last. Throughout the nineteenth century emissaries extended Britain's sway over the continent. The typical approach was to invite a local ruler to sign a treaty that exchanged a small gift of arms or trade goods for the right to exploit minerals or other wealth. Invariably, however, Britain felt it must protect that right, and exploitation soon turned into rule. Addressing one case where protection was deemed necessary, Britain's Lord

Salisbury wrote caustically that, "We need not discuss the principles. . . They amount to this, that when a merchant differs from a native chief as to their respective rights, the native chief is to be deported." Nowhere was this ideal more dramatically demonstrated than along Great Fish River in 1847, when one Sir Harry Smith invited a group of Xhosa chiefs to witness the blowing-up of a gunpowder-packed wagon. "There go the treaties," he shouted. "Do you hear? No more treaties!" He then told them their land was under British sovereignty. What could they do but submit? Others took a more oblique approach. The result was the same. "Did you ever see a chameleon catch a fly?" asked Lobengula, king of the Matabele. "England is the chameleon and I am the fly."

One by one most of the European nations rushed to grab a "place in the sun"—as Germany's kaiser put it—until almost the whole continent was under white rule. In 1884, at the Congress of Berlin, European leaders met to settle their differences. Lines were drawn, stakes were claimed, and

March of the Warriors

During the 1800s southern Africa was shaken by massive population shifts. The mfecane, *or "crushing," initiated by the Zulu was followed by the migratory Great Trek of the Boers.*

The explosive growth of the *mfecane* is believed to have resulted in a million dead Africans. Zulu warrior necklace.

At the dawn of the nineteenth century, Natal had too many people living off too few acres. The Zulu clans grouped together and power centralized under a chief named Dingiswayo. He put his people on a war footing and created an army comprising regiments, or *impis*. Under his leadership and that of Shaka, his successor, the Zulu conquered adjacent territories and provoked mayhem. Unable to resist, neighboring peoples broke over the Drakensberg Mountains onto the high veldt. The effect was terrible; peoples who had hitherto lived in peace now had to fight for survival. Widespread famine resulted from a collapse in farming.

Some peoples never returned to their ancestral territories. Among them were the Shona and Matabele who eventually dominated Zimbabwe.

This great dispersal was echoed by the Boers, the white farmers of the Cape. Between 1836 and 1838 they moved northward to escape British rule. Some pushed into the high veldt, others looped down into Natal where, in December 1838 at the Battle of Blood River, 600 Boer settlers armed with rifles decimated an army of 12,000 spear-wielding Zulu warriors.

Taken together, the *mfecane* and the Great Trek—as the Boers called their migration—completely changed the face of southern Africa.

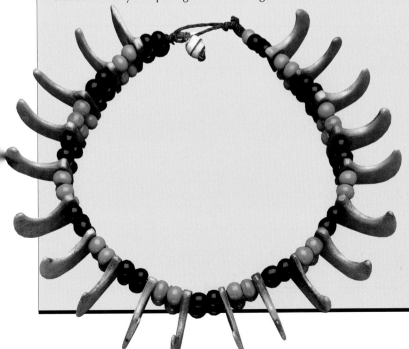

spheres of influence were agreed. "We have been engaged in drawing lines upon maps where no white man's foot has ever trod," remarked Lord Salisbury. The result was a set of boundaries that owed everything to European interests, a little to topography, and nothing to African reality. These boundaries enclosed the states that comprise modern Africa. Today, their inhabitants are still coming to terms with their contrived nationhood.

Broken Spirits?

Temporal and spiritual colonization went hand in hand. With the exception of the Sahel, Ethiopia, and the Swahili regions, which had all long been influenced by Christianity and Islam, the bulk of Africa was animistic. Spirits ruled the world and could be found anywhere—in a rock, a stream, a cave, or an animal. Often the spirits were those of human ancestors and their propitiation took the form of song, dance, and sacrifices—occasionally, of humans. "Witch-doctors," as Westerners called them, mediated between the tangible and the spirit worlds, conducting rituals and advising people on the proper steps whereby they could achieve fertility, ensure agricultural prosperity or, perhaps, banish the ghost of a slain enemy.

Introduced through the medium of evangelical missionaries, the Christian God was absorbed readily enough into the system, albeit with some misgivings. The message of equality for all men and women, for example, did not accord with the realities of African life—it did not reflect the current state of European society either, but this was passed

The introduction of the Bible and the Koran marked a profound transformation of Africa's oral cultures. Carved missionary figure, Congo, 19th century.

over. Many rulers worried that the new deity might bring political upset. The witch-doctors too, who were often held in much greater respect than the chiefs, feared for their standing in society.

Generally, however, it was not so much Christianity that was viewed askance as what it brought in its wake. It often happened that missionaries—such as the celebrated Scottish explorer Dr. David Livingstone—were the vanguard of Western depredation. In their search for souls to save they opened up hitherto unknown areas of Africa and in doing so brought them to the attention of less benevolent interests. Acting from the best of motives and frequently enduring great hardships to impart their message, the missionaries nevertheless went down in African folklore as the harbingers of doom. "They had the Bible and we had the land," ran a common saying. "Now they have the land and we have the Bible."

Emperor Theodore of Ethiopia, meanwhile, expressed the mechanics of colonialism in blunt terms. "I know their game," he said. "First it's traders and missionaries. Then it's ambassadors. After that they bring the guns. We shall do better to go straight to the guns."

Ethiopia was the only African state that had sufficient guns to thwart the colonial impetus. Most of the continent succumbed to Western rule and economic methods. Throughout the nineteenth and twentieth centuries traditional agriculture was replaced by cash crops such as sugar, tea, and coffee. The idea was that with enough cash—hence the name—Africans would no longer need to be self-sufficient but could afford to buy foreign produce. The idea, however, ignored the fact that when markets dipped the crops did not sell and Africans received no cash. In the absence of homegrown food they became ever more dependent on imports

they could not pay for. Independence following World War II did little to set matters right.

The entire process was encapsulated in the words of the British empire-builder H.M. Stanley. Having stormed his way through the Congo basin in the 1880s, he declared that he detested the whole continent. But maybe something could be made of it. What he wanted, he said, was "to put the civilisation of Europe into the barbarism of Africa." To prove his ideals he amassed some 400 treaties to create the Congo Free State for King Leopold II of Belgium. Administered as the king's personal fiefdom, the territory became a byword for brutality, seemingly epitomizing the fact that Europe had brought Africa not civilization but a new concept of barbarism.

Once Western influence had established itself, there was no turning back the clock. Divided into unfamiliar states, saddled with a dependent economic system and sometimes totally dispossessed—as under South Africa's apartheid system—

A funeral procession for a fisherman in Ghana. His coffin in the shape of a tsile fish has been daubed with the blood of a sacrificed sheep. The use of coffins to reflect the occupation or character of the deceased is a popular one in Ghana and shows that distinctive African tradition is still alive and well.

Africans struggled to make sense of the new order. The seemingly endless succession of wars that have bedeviled the continent in recent decades—arguably a direct legacy of colonial rule—suggest that the struggle is still continuing. And yet, for all that Africa has been turned on its head, it retains its distinctive identity. Beneath the veneer of Western civilization, the old ways still exist. The mountains, forests, and rivers are still there; so is the wildlife—albeit in diminished numbers; the hunter-gatherers and pastoralists follow their traditional lifestyles; and the ancient mythologies that underpin African life continue to flourish. Africa has absorbed the outside world. But it has not succumbed to it.

23

ANCIENT PALACES OF THE KINGS

*Z*imbabwe is a Shona word for a walled stone enclosure built for a king. From about the eighth century onward hundreds of these "sacred houses" were erected throughout the kingdoms of the gold-rich lands along the eastern part of the Zambezi River. They appear to have been abandoned in the early nineteenth century, although the exact reasons why remain a mystery—very likely the inability of the surrounding land to continue to support the grazing cattle of the royal court. Great Zimbabwe, the largest ancient stone construction south of the Sahara, was the domestic and ceremonial centerpiece of the Monomotapa empire.

Above: The Western Enclosure forms part of the hill-located complex, the third element accompanying the Great Enclosure and the valley ruins outside it. Within all the walled areas would have stood mud and thatch buildings.

Right: Soapstone carving of a raptor dating from 1200–1400 CE. The figure may once have graced the Eastern Enclosure wall, representing a mythical messenger between humankind and the gods above.

Left: The conical tower of Great Zimbabwe dates from the period of Rozwi hegemony, c.1500. This last phase reflects East African influences as a result of the coastal-inland gold and spice trades.

Right: The massive stone walls and narrow passage that separate the inner and outer walls of the Great Enclosure.

Above: The Great Enclosure of Great Zimbabwe, near Masvingo, is the best known of southern Africa's many stone fortresses. Construction commenced in the early 12th century, but the later acropolis building dates from c.1500.

Right: The stonework at the site makes much use of patterning, and on occasion color. Some experts believe this may conceal a sexual symbolism; the turrets and this chevron pattern, for example, may both represent young men.

WONDERS OF CREATION

The San or Bushmen of the Kalahari Desert in southern Africa tell of a creator named Dxui, the first spirit who made all things. Dxui took many forms, sometimes appearing as a flower, sometimes as a tree; he could be a man or a bird, a busy fly, or the rippling water of life; the final form he took was that of a lizard, said by the San to be the oldest of all creatures. The San's contention that the creator was once present in the world, pervading his handiwork, crops up often in the highly various myths of creation and human origins told by the peoples of Africa.

A number of the myths also seek to explain why the divine is now inaccessible to mortals, suggesting that the god—sometimes a single supreme being predating any Islamic or Christian influence—who once lived happily among the peoples he had created was driven away by their bad behavior and hid himself somewhere humans could not follow—often in the sky. According to other mythologies, to be sure, there were many gods and they always lived in the sky, from where they descended to make the Earth. Olodumare ("Owner of the Limitless Spaces"), the supreme sky god of Nigeria's Yoruba, sent his sons Obatala and Oduduwa down from Heaven (see pages 34–35). Mawu-Lisa, androgynous creator divinity of the Fon people with one body and two faces, was another great sky deity who gave issue to many divinities, some of whom descended to the Earth below. The Fon and Yoruba traditions have large pantheons of gods and goddesses, but in both it is clear that many of the lesser deities—*voduns* for the Fon, *orishas* for the Yoruba—originated on Earth. Scholars speculate that some of these can be traced to ancestral kings or warriors, who were deified after their death.

For peoples in most parts of Africa ancestors were worthy of deepest reverence, symbolizing the bond that united the people. Traditionally the belief was that ancestors lived on invisibly and wielded great influence over visible reality; they had to be worshipped and placated. The ancestors also often represented the furthest limit of mythical curiosity. Many African peoples took part in great migrations over centuries and preserved their tribal memory in myths: but they kept no history of humankind beyond their own first days. For these peoples, creation myths were stories not of the first humans, but of the emergence of their people or kingdom.

Opposite: **An acacia tree amid the rich colors of the Namib Desert, a symbol of life and growth in a harsh environment.**

Above: **Lizards were believed by some African peoples to be the most ancient of creatures. These reptilian protective designs were painted on cloth by Senufo hunters from the Ivory Coast.**

27

Oldest Tales of the San

The ancient creation myths of the San or Bushmen of the Kalahari Desert connect to a primeval era of irregular light and nights of total darkness. Their stories explain the first appearance of the antelopes and account for the arrival of the sun and moon in the sky.

The San's hunting lifestyle is representative of that of the earliest humans in Africa, intimate with the bush and the antelopes—springboks and heavier elands—that are among their prey. San mythology has central roles for the animals and insects of the bush, notably the praying mantis, a divine creator in many San myths.

According to San lore, the sacred mantis was married to the hyrax, a small mammal, and their daughter was the porcupine. In one story, the porcupine was the wife of Kwammang-a, a primeval ancestor whose discarded sandal the mantis used to create the first eland for the hungry San to hunt.

The mantis kept the eland in a cool water pool surrounded by thick reeds, and brought it honey for food. Slowly the eland grew stronger and bigger until it was the size of a brawny ox. One day a young hunter went with the mantis to the waterhole and spied with the divine insect on this strange creature. Then Kwammang-a, hearing the hunter's account of what he had seen, took his bow and followed the path to the waterhole. In time the eland emerged cautiously from the reeds to drink and Kwammang-a fired a deadly arrow that brought the beast down. The mantis, far away seeking food for the eland, found that the honey had dried up and knew this to be a sign that blood had been spilled on the thirsty ground and that his majestic antelope had been brought to an evil end.

He hurried to the waterhole, but when he called the eland it did not come, and the mantis wept. A dusty trail of blood led him to where the hunters were cutting up the beast for meat. Rage swept through the mantis and he tried to shoot the hunters with his own arrows. But all his shots missed and somehow came back toward him.

In the bush the mantis found the dead eland's thrown-away gall bladder hanging from a branch. When he split it open blackness flooded every-

Ancient San rock art from Kamberg, South Africa, of a hornless, heavily built eland antelope and human hunter figure.

How Things Got Their Colors

The sacred mantis brought honey to many antelopes, and according to the type of honey the animals took their varied colors. To the upper rim of the rainbow the mantis gave his own hue.

The mantis brought honey to the first eland both as food (see main text) and as a refreshing balm. When he visited the eland in the sweetness of evening he would mix some of the honey with water and use the concoction to rub down the quivering sides of the great beast he had created. The eland has a dark fawn coloring because the mantis gave it dark-colored wasps' honey.

The mantis brought light-colored liquid honey to the gemsbok, and the animal is therefore white. The hartebeest was fed on the reddish comb of young bees; although the hartebeests of central and western Africa are brown, those in southern Africa are red. Brownish honey also accounted for the dark skin of the now

extinct quagga, once a member of the zebra family. Springboks typically have a red-fawn coat because like the hartebeest they ate the honey of young bees.

Meanwhile, according to the San, in the colors of the rainbow yellow appears to arch over red because the yellow mantis lies above the red-brown of their ancestor Kwammang-a. In this instance the mantis is ascribed a yellow color, although most of the insects are green or brown in order to blend in with the foliage on which they perch, invisibly waiting for prey. However, there is one exotic species of African mantis with green-yellow wing markings that appear like eyes when it spreads its wings. The rainbow itself was sometimes called Kwammang-a.

where, driving the bright sun beneath the horizon. The mantis himself could not see momentarily and blundered into bushes. Once recovered, he took the gall bladder and threw it up into the sky—and it became the moon, which illumines the darkness of night for the good of the hunters.

When Sun Lived on Earth

The San also told a tale of the sun's first appearance in the sky. In the earliest days the sun lived among the tribes of the bush. He was like other men except that a brilliant light shone from his armpits when he raised his arms; then when he let

his arms fall again, darkness swept across the Earth. A wise old woman instructed her grandchildren to creep up on old man Sun and hurl him into the sky so that the light he released could fall far and wide on all living things.

They waited until Sun had lain on the ground to sleep, then they crept toward him stealthily and in an instant they had seized him and flung him up high over their heads into the great cavern of the sky. They called out to him to stay put and to descend no more to Earth. Far away, across the bush, the children's relatives saw Sun appear as a golden sphere in the heavens and were pleased. Thus darkness was driven from the skies.

29

The Separation of Heaven and Earth

African peoples separated from one another by thousands of miles tell remarkably similar tales of how the sky and Earth were once close together. The story of why the sky withdrew to a great distance is popular in their oral traditions—and often explains why the sky deity or the creator god who lives in or beyond the sky is now distant from his people.

A myth told in western Africa from Nigeria to the Ivory Coast links the remoteness of the sky to the apparent inaccessibility of the divine. According to this tale, the great creator god once lived close to his people, just beyond the sky that rested a little way above their heads. But the people, becoming accustomed to their good fortune, began to mistreat the sky: at the cooking pot, women would reach up and seize a piece of the blue heaven to add to their soups, while after the meal children would scrabble among the clouds to clean the grease from their hands.

Traditionally African women used long pestles to pound their cereal in a deep mortar carved from a log. When the women were particularly energetic their pestles would sometimes bump into the clouds and sky. One woman often hit the creator. One day, as she was working out her frustrations on the grain, she gave the deity an almighty blow in the eye and he rose up in fury, rushing away to the inaccessible place where he now lives. In that instant the sky also swept upward to its present position. The woman who had inadvertently driven God away gathered her children and instructed them to collect wooden mortars far and wide; her plan was to build a tower tall enough to reach his new celestial home. The

An Ashanti brass weight depicts women using a pestle to pound cereal. It would actually have been used to measure gold.

A misty Mount Kilimanjaro dominates the savanna, evoking the days when the heavenly clouds hung low over the Earth.

audacious attempt almost succeeded, but the tower was too short. Then the woman, desperate to succeed, told her children to pull the lowest mortar from the tower so that they could add it to the top. The tower crashed down, flinging the men and women who clung to it to a painful death.

In a similar myth related among the Nuba of eastern Sudan, it was said that during the first days the sky hung so low over the Earth that men and women could touch it—and sometimes its near presence became too much to bear. Women beating their millet in a bowl found they could not stir freely without catching on the sky; they were burned because the sky prevented them lifting their hands away from the cooking pots. Once a woman lost her temper and stabbed upward with her spoon. The handle ripped through the clouds, making a gash in the heavens—and the sky, offended, swept away upward to form a great arch over the lowly Earth. In another account the sky was angered because in hard times people would rip rough pieces off the clouds in order to satisfy the cravings of their hunger.

Both these tales involve the necessary human activity of food preparation and can be interpreted as harking back to a golden age when survival came easy, attributing the troubling remoteness of the creator to human actions and laziness. In the Sudan a similar myth told by the Dinka relates how in the first days the creator god lived close to his people and life was trouble-free—but he swiftly withdrew when they offended him. When the great god lived in the sky just over people's heads, sickness and death were unknown in the lands of Africa. God even allowed a rope to hang down to Earth so that his creatures could easily ascend to see him. The deity provided the first people with just a single grain of millet each day but it was enough for their needs and they did not have to labor on the land. One day, however, the first woman tried to use more grain than she was allowed and in pounding it she clattered into the sky with her pestle. God swept away in a fury, the rope to Heaven was cut, the sky rose far away from the land, and sickness and death were unleashed to satisfy their dread hunger on Earth. The Dinka were pastoralists surviving in dusty, infertile country; by ancestral tradition it was not right for one family or individual to have more than others. This ancient conviction surely informs the mythical account—for the woman's desire for more than she actually needs is severely punished.

Heavenly Thread

A common theme in many African cultures is that of a rope or thread linking Heaven and Earth and providing a means of communication for the celestial deity. In addition, however, it also offers an escape route (see page 39). In Sierra Leone the

Mende told how the creator god departed from Earth because his creatures were too insistent in their demands. He made all things—the pounding ocean and the great forest trees; the fierce beasts of prey and the trumpeting elephants; the leaping fish, and the clever spider. But his last creation, men and women, caused him a good deal of trouble for they often came to ask him for things. The creator did not mind supplying what his creatures wanted, but the first people asked for so much and so often that in time he grew tired of them.

In the calm of deep night, when the fretful mortals had settled down to rest, God silently and gently took himself away. When the people woke they looked frenziedly about for God in his usual places but they could not find him. Then, they saw him in every distant direction, all around them in the land and its vegetation, in the roaring waters, the rolling thunderclouds, the steep air. God bade them farewell and left a second time to settle up at the top of the arching sky. As a parting gift he bestowed a fowl on every man and woman so that people could humbly make sacrifices to this once familiar God who had removed himself into distant grandeur.

In a myth of the Lozi people of Zambia and Zimbabwe, God also fled to escape the attentions of humans. In the earliest days, they say, God lived

Tales of Other Worlds

Many African peoples tell tales of a traveler's voyage to the lands of the dead. For some cultures, including the Ashanti of Ghana, the spirit world exists in a hidden dimension alongside that of the everyday; for others, such as the Wacaga of southern Africa, the spirits inhabit an underworld.

Young Ashanti Kwasi Benefo lost four wives, one after the other, to the cold ogre Death. Each time grief stunned him, but he dutifully prepared his wife for burial, dressing her in beads and an *amoasie* or silk loincloth— for the elders taught that the souls of the dead needed these precious goods to pay their way across the river between the land of the living and the home of the tribe's ancestors.

Eventually he decided he wanted to follow them all to Asamando, the Land of the Dead. He walked to the forest place where the dead were buried, then on through darkness and in utter silence across a barren land suffused with pale light. He came to a deep river

and saw an old woman with a brass pot full of *amoasies*. At first she refused to let Kwasi cross to the land of the dead, but finally she took pity on him and made a ford in the river. He walked on and came to a village. Here he could see huts and dry ground as at home but no people—for its inhabitants were invisible as the air itself. He heard his four wives' voices welcome him, and felt them bathe his feet. They sang him gentle songs, then told him to return home, marry once more, and live out his life; when his time came to die, they would be waiting to welcome him. When Kwasi awoke he was back in the forest near his village. He married a fifth time and lived into ripe old age.

In a Wacaga tale the spirit world was entirely different. A girl named Marwe fled from a family quarrel and won great riches in the land of the dead. Escaping her father's anger, Marwe jumped into a pond and found her way to the spirit world through a hole in the bottom of the pool. There she met other children and worked in the fields for an old woman.

In time she began to long for home and told the woman she wanted to return to the land of the living. The old woman ordered her to plunge her hands into a pot and, when Marwe did so, her arms and wrists were covered with precious bangles. She did the same with her legs, and pretty copper chains with a wife on Earth but was surprised in his worldly home by a quick-witted and persistent man named Kamonu, who was distressed that his child had died. God was determined to keep his dwelling place secret so he fled to a river island. When Kamonu discovered him there, too, he chose a giddy mountain peak for his dwelling place, but Kamonu followed him. Above all else God craved privacy and solitude, but everywhere he looked there were people—settling along the rivers, in the forests and on the savannas, filling the great land of Africa with children. Then, God called a flock of darting, chattering birds together and instructed them to fan out across the continent in order to find him a refuge where men like Kamonu could never track him. They were unable to do it, so God chose a wise wagtail from the flock to perform a divination and find a safe place. The wagtail did so and advised consulting the spider, who can spin a strong thread across empty air. The spider cast a delicate rope up from Earth to the top of the sky, and God and his wife climbed far from troublesome humankind. There they live in peace. Kamonu and his companions, of course, did not know that they were beaten and tried ambitiously to reach Heaven by building a tower from tree trunks, but the construction collapsed and many were killed.

covered her ankles and feet. Then, the old woman dressed Marwe in a beaded petticoat and told her that her husband on Earth would be a young man named Sawoye.

The old woman guided Marwe back to the pond and left her on the bank. She was a ravishing sight with her fine features, delicate petticoat, and glittering jewelry. The local people came to see their newly returned neighbor and the chieftain asked her to be his bride. But she refused. Then came a young man named Sawoye, whose face was badly marked by a skin disease. At once Marwe announced that he was to be her husband. Sawoye carried her home and they lived happily as man and wife in great prosperity.

Kwasi Benefo approaches the spirit woman at the river he needs to cross to be reunited with his wives in Asamando, the Land of the Dead.

Making the Earth

The great mystery of how Earth, sky, and ocean emerged at the beginning of time is linked in many African cultures with the first days of the tribe.

Nigeria's Yoruba people have a highly developed mythology of the creation of the world and of the kingdoms of Yoruba, with many versions featuring different members of a pantheon of spirits and gods. In one important myth, the great god of the sky Olodumare—or Olorun—looked down from his seat in the heavens and saw that the world was no more than a vast ocean. He summoned two of his sons, Obatala and Oduduwa, gave them a bag, a hen, and a chameleon, and sent them down to the world. As they descended he lowered a great palm tree that settled on the waters: when the brothers landed, they did so in the tree's branches.

Almost at once Obatala began hacking at the bark of the tree and made a strong palm wine from its sweet sap. He soon became drunk and fell asleep. Oduduwa, meanwhile, climbed down and opened the bag his father had given him. Inside he discovered sand, which he sprinkled on the heaving surface of the water. Then he released the chameleon onto the sand; the creature advanced very slowly—as chameleons have ever since—and the land held firm. Looking deeper in the bag, Oduduwa found some dark earth, which he scattered over the sand. He placed the hen down on it and this animal, scratching and pecking, flung the earth far and wide, where it settled to form the great continent of Africa.

Oduduwa walked proudly into his territory. From up high Olodumare dispatched Aje ("Wealth" or "Prosperity") to be Oduduwa's wordly companion. Olodumare also gave his son a sack of maize to sow in the ground, a supply of cowrie shells for him to use in trade with other peoples, and three bars of iron to be made into weapons and agricultural tools. Proud Oduduwa was the first king of

A sacred palm tree depicted in 17th-century Yoruba brasswork. Their creator of Earth varied depending on the story, it could be Obatala or Oduduwa, sometimes Oranmiyan and even Ogun.

Yoruba. He called the place where he had performed his act of creation Ile-Ife or "Wide House"—and it became a great city of the Yoruba.

Yoruba Created to Rule

Another version explained more explicitly why the Yoruba should exercise power over other peoples. In his great realm of the sky Olodumare created seven princes, then gave them a chicken, twenty iron bars, bags containing cowrie shells, beads, and a mysterious substance wrapped in cloth. He sent them down to the world and, once again, created a great palm tree in which they landed. The six oldest princes—Olowu, Onisabe, Orangun, Oni, Ajero, and Alaketu—took what they thought was valuable from the gifts of the sky god and left the youngest prince, Oranmiyan, with the chicken, the iron bars, and the substance wrapped in cloth. Then they were gone, back to the heavens.

Opening the cloth, Oranmiyan found a black powder and threw it on the waters beneath the tree. The chicken at once flew down, and scattered it far and wide to make the land. When Oranmiyan settled in the land, the six older princes reappeared and demanded their share of the new world—but Oranmiyan refused, showing them the iron bars that he had transformed into an awesome array of weapons. The six princes bowed low and Oranmiyan graciously granted them a small portion of the new land to rule, but only on the condition that they and their descendants would be subject to his descendants for all time. So Oranmiyan, in this version the first king of the Yoruba, established the greatness of that tribe in the very first days of history. In some traditions he is known as Oranyan and is said like King Arthur in Britain to be living still, sleeping until a time of great trouble for the Yoruba when he will rise up in their defense (see pages 118–120).

The Shape of the Universe

Some African peoples understand the universe to be shaped like everyday objects such as a gourd or an egg.

To many cultures, the round calabash illustrates the shape of the universe.

The Fon people who founded the seventeenth-century kingdom of Dahomey (modern West Africa's Benin) saw the universe as resembling a split calabash, a round fruit whose hard skin can be used as a container for water or seeds.

The Fon used the image of a calabash cut in half horizontally to describe the universe: the top half contains the sky, sun, and moon and the bottom half is full of water. The Earth, they said, is flat and floats in the waters held in the bottom half. For this reason, when people dig in the earth, they eventually hit water.

The top half of the universe rests on the bottom half, and the two halves meet at the horizon where sea and sky touch, in a wonderful place that people can never reach, no matter how far they sail. In the dawn of the world the creator placed a sacred snake around the calabash to bind the two halves. In some accounts, however, the divine serpent Aido-Hwedo lies beneath the Earth to prevent it from sinking (see page 48).

The Dogon of Mali believe that the creator Amma took the shape of an egg (see page 36) and, according to one myth, he made the universe in the same form—as his twin. Within the egg were four elemental parts and the divisions between the parts were the four directions of space. Altars to Amma are made of a vertical stone built up with clay into an egg shape. "Amma" means "to hold firm and keep in place" and one who repeats the name helps to maintain and sustain the universe.

Life Bursts Forth

The Kuba, who live in the abundant rainforest of Central Africa, call their creator god Mbombo and picture creation as a sudden eruption from his mouth. Once, according to their account, nothing existed but restless water lost in darkness—and Mbombo, a spirit who moved over the water. Then, in the deep, dark hours of the first day, Mbombo was stricken by a sharp stomach pain and vomited, producing the sun, moon, and a stream of bright stars. Light fell all around him. As the sun shone, the ocean became clouds and the water level fell, revealing hills and plains. Again Mbombo's stomach convulsed, this time sending forth a wonderful and various stream of life: the tall sky, the sharp-forked lightning, deep-rooted trees, animals in all their lithe power, and the first man and woman.

The Yoruba god Obatala, who failed in his mission to create land on Earth because he fell into a drunken dream, was credited with creating the sun. When the king of a forest tribe neglected to make the correct sacrifices, the gods sent a tree crashing down to destroy his house—but Obatala intervened, using divine magic to transform the wood into gold. He ordered the heavenly smith to make a boat and jar from the gold, then commanded his slave to take up the jar, climb into the glittering boat, and pilot it up to the peak of Heaven and on to the far horizon. He watched with great satisfaction as the sun journeyed across Heaven for the first time. His father Olodumare, lord of the sky, decreed that the gentle moon should rise to complement the sun in the sky. Olodumare fashioned the pale moon as a flintstone with one thin and one rounded aspect. As it spins, ever obedient to Olodumare's command, it presents itself to the peoples of Yoruba in different aspects, from crescent to full.

The Power of Amma

The Dogon of Mali in West Africa revere a single god, Amma, who created all things. At the beginning of time he existed in the form of a great egg that contained the entire creation in potential form. The egg contained the elements fire, earth, water, and air, and in a series of seven explosions these combined to make life. When the elements act upon one another life follows—for instance, air blowing on fire creates sparks, while water falling on earth will make plants grow. In one account of the creation Amma first designed the universe in his thoughts and drew a series of signs in space with water; then he sent forth the signs and they took form, becoming real. In another version, Amma's act of creation was likened to that of a potter. He cast the sun and the moon as pots and hung them in the sky;

A Dogon altar iron in the form of a dancing figure, used in ancestor worship. The first human blacksmith was a Dogon ancestor who had stolen a fragment of the sun from the heavenly smithy of the Nummo spirit twins.

afterward, he took a handful of small clay pieces and hurled them into space, creating the stars. The Earth he made female, also from clay, and laid her out flat, face upward. Dogon craftsmen—especially ironworkers and blacksmiths—were held in the highest regard. Traditionally, they were not required to work the land, but were given food at harvest time; the iron they smelted provided a significant commodity to trade with.

The Power of Rain

Essential for agriculture, the regulation of life-giving water is overwhelmingly important. In a Fon tale of quarrels between the gods, the thunder god Hevioso refused to send rains to feed the crops until the Earth deity Sagbata accepted his authority to rule the sky without interference.

Sagbata was a son of the androgynous two-headed creator Mawu-Lisa (see page 41); Hevioso, also male and female, was his brother-sister. According to one tale, Sagbata was sold into slavery by Mawu-Lisa and became Death's servant. He survived the ordeal and was sold on to another owner, but when he eventually escaped from slavery and returned home, he discovered that Hevioso had been made king of the tribe. The siblings quarrelled and Sagbata seized power from Hevioso, who took himself off to the sky.

Sagbata ordered his people to raise great crops of corn, but Hevioso looked down from the sky and resolved to withhold the rains. When the wet season was due and no waters fell from Heaven to soften the hard ground, famine spread and many died. Then the people began to complain to Sagbata and the Earth deity saw that he had to act swiftly.

Sagbata called together all the peoples and animals of his kingdom. As his subjects watched, he took threads of black and white cotton, raised them to his mouth, whispered a soft command and then set the threads hanging in the sky as a ladder between Earth and Heaven. Then he asked for volunteers to climb up to Hevioso and demand that the rains be restored. The eagle was the first to go: it soared halfway up the sky but then was struck down by Hevioso. Next the cat tried, but when it reached the same halfway point, Hevioso dispatched it with a thunderbolt.

At last it was the turn of the slow, sure chameleon—favored creature of Lisa, the male half of Mawu-Lisa. The chameleon climbed so slowly that Hevioso grew bored and went away to deal with other matters. From time to time, Hevioso returned and flung a rasping thunderbolt down at the poor creature, but the chameleon hid behind the thread to which it clung. Finally, the chameleon stood outside Hevioso's dwelling. He passed on Sagbata's message begging for rain—and Hevioso, seeing that Sagbata was accepting his authority in Heaven, relented. Rain fell, and in Sagbata's land the corn grew tall. Some say that Sagbata had to submit entirely to Hevioso because the thunder god had possession of the two things essential to life on Earth: the water of the rains and the fire of celestial lightning.

Ancestors of Humankind

A great range of myths, all highly colored by natural conditions and different peoples' ways of life, describe how the first men and women were made or came into being. Again and again the father and mother of the race were said to be made from local materials or to have emerged from a particular local feature.

The Shilluk, whose home borders the Nile River in southern Sudan, say that the creator god Juok made humans out of river mud—and their myth cleverly accounts for the different shades of people's skins. Juok on his travels found black, brown, and white muds: with the black mud he made dark-skinned Africans; with the brown he made the tan-complexioned Arabs; and with the white mud, white men and women from the north. He planned a good life for his creatures, giving them long legs for walking and running in the river shallows, long arms for using the hoe in the fields by the Nile, fast tongues to shape words and make resonant songs, and sensitive ears so that they could delight in music.

Clay, Water, and Crafty Chameleons

A story of the Pangwe people of what is now Cameroon accords with the theory of evolution, asserting that human life developed out of the water, in which, deep in the past, people lived like reptiles. They too said that the creator fashioned the first being out of clay, but in their story this primeval being was a lizard. With delicate touch, the creator formed the lizard then laid it gently in water. After seven days, having been commanded to emerge from the pool, the lizard transformed itself into a human and clambered out onto land.

The Yao, settlers on the banks of Lake Malawi in eastern Africa, tell how the first people came from the ever-moving waters and claim that humankind's creation was a disaster for a previously harmonious world. When history was young, the creator god Mulungu lived on Earth with the many quick-witted creatures of the wild. There were no people, but neither was there conflict or cruelty. Then the crafty chameleon devised a fish trap and lowered it into the water, bringing about a disturbing change. The first time he returned to the trap he found it heavy with fish and he feasted on his haul; the second time, it was empty; the third time, he was intrigued to find a miniature man and woman in the trap.

The chameleon did not know what these strange creatures were, and took them to Mulungu. The creator studied the tiny people, then instructed the chameleon to release them, declaring that they would grow as they walked about. The chameleon opened the trap as instructed and, sure enough, the man and woman grew to normal size. But almost at once they brought destruction to Mulungu's peaceful creation.

Seizing two sticks, they started a fire but were careless. The flames spread through the entire forest, driving the animals to desperate flight. The man and woman took advantage of the animals' panic to trap and kill a buffalo, then roasted its flesh in the fire and ate it. They were enraptured by the taste and each day afterward started a fire and slaughtered another of Mulungu's beasts. The creator was deeply distressed but did not know how to stop them.

In the forest the animals fled for their lives. The chameleon climbed to the top of a tree, and from this vantage point the busily destructive people looked no bigger than they had when confined in his fish trap. The spider flung out a strong rope of thread and climbed so high into the sky that it disappeared. Mulungu saw it go and decided to flee himself. He called out in his anguish to the spider, asking it how it had scaled the smooth blue of the sky. The spider sent down a thread to the creator, who left the Earth to settle in the heavens.

Reed People

A great many myths suggest that the first humans emerged from the ground or from plants. The Zulu of southern Africa share a story with the Tsonga people of modern-day Mozambique that claims that the first man came out of a reed or a bed of reeds. According to the Tsonga version, the bird god N'wari alighted one day on a fertile riverbank, used its bill to make a hole in a reed there, and in the hole laid an egg. In due time the reed burst open and produced the first man, who built himself a hut of mud and grass. He later met a woman, whose origins are not explained, and they gave issue to many strong-legged children.

The Herero people of Namibia, who traditionally lived by stock-breeding, said the first people and their cattle climbed down from a tree that stands even today deep in the veldt. They also say that their neighbors, the San, emerged from a hole in the ground. Far away in western Africa, the Ashanti agree that the first people and animals came from deep in the earth. One night a worm made a hole in the surface of the Earth and from this came a dog, men and women, and the proud leopard, which is sacred to some Ashanti. The first people were terrified by their unknown surroundings, but their leader was able to calm them.

Enjoying a vantage point like the one it secured to escape the destructive activity of the first people, the chameleon sits on top of this dance mask from Cameroon. Found throughout Africa, the reptile has a reputation for wisdom.

39

The Heavenly Blacksmith

In African mythology a divine blacksmith often plays a crucial role in preparing the universe for humanity. He is commonly described as descending from the sky.

According to the Fon people of Benin in West Africa the eldest son of Mawu-Lisa, the twin creator divinities, was Gu, the heavenly blacksmith. He was brought down to Earth by Lisa, the male twin, in the form of a ceremonial iron sword that Lisa held in his hand. It is said that Gu was then charged with making Earth habitable for humans, a task he has never given up. Gu taught ironworking and showed people how to fashion tools so that they could obtain food, cover their bodies, and build shelters.

Amma, the creator god of the Dogon (who believed that creation began with an egg that was the seed of the cosmos, vibrating seven times and bursting open to reveal five Nommo spirit pairs), made the first spirit blacksmith from the placenta of a Nommo. But this spirit had no fire, so he stole a piece of the sun from the heavenly Nommo twins and came down from heaven to Earth in a celestial ark. Other Myths of the Sahara region relate how the first blacksmith made a hoe from the skull of a heavenly antelope called Bintu, then descended to Earth with it in order to teach the newly created human race how to cultivate.

Unfortunately, he was crushed by a falling tree as they set about building a town, but the people completed the settlement. Subsequently the creator god encountered them and chose one of the first Ashanti to be his personal helper.

People of the Sacred Tree

The pygmies, who live as hunters deep in the forests of Central Africa, traced their origins to a sacred tree, according to one tradition. It was the smooth-backed chameleon that freed them to roam the forests. The chameleon was going about its business when it heard a sound like running water or softly singing birds, apparently coming from inside a broad tree trunk. Its curiosity was aroused, for at that time there was no water anywhere on Earth. The reptile hacked the tree open with a blade and a great flood poured out that reached to the far corners of the Earth. The first man and woman, both light-skinned pygmies, were borne out on the waters. They settled in the forest as man and wife and from them issued the entire race of pygmies.

Another pygmy myth told that the first man, named Efe, was a hunter of such great prowess that the creator snatched him up to Heaven to scour the dense forests and wide plains of the divine realm for game. He gave Efe three marvellous spears and sent him off to hunt.

Pygmies are expert hunters of the elephant—it is difficult for the massive, slow-moving beast to strike them because they are short and swift. Their ancestral champion was no different and Efe killed a great heavenly elephant and won rapturous acclaim among the sky-dwellers. After a long time he was sent back to Earth, but he had changed considerably during his sojourn in the sky and his people—who had long ago presumed him to be dead—could not recognize him. At length Efe's brother knew him and then the great hunter, forefather of the race, was warmly welcomed by his descendants in the forest.

First Days of Faith

In other places, myths of human origins are tied to the establishment of a people's religious faith. In one Fon tradition, the first humans to appear in the lands of Dahomey were worshippers of the creator goddess-god Mawu-Lisa. The original man and woman came down from the sky in the course of a heavy rainstorm. The torrential rains continued for seventeen days while the first people chanted the name of their deity Sogbo, who had sent them down to Earth.

Seven days into this seemingly endless rainstorm, a second couple were washed down from the sky. They were adorned with beads called *lisaje* ("Lisa's beads") and were worshippers of Mawu-Lisa; in Adja they raised the first temple dedicated to the creator deity. The couple planned a sacrifice to Mawu-Lisa and on the appointed day the rains came once again, this time bringing down a crowd of people to help in the act of worship. Then, when the sacrifice was complete, the helpers returned to Heaven.

In due course the man and woman erected four temples: one for Mawu, one for Lisa, the third for the war deity Gu, and the last for Age, divinity of hunting. They established the correct sacrifices for the different gods and goddesses: at Lisa's temple, white goats and white chickens were sacrificed, Mawu was honored with sheep, Gu received white roosters and Age, dogs. Then the man and woman who had come down from Heaven with the *lisaje* beads returned to the sky. They left the beads and a daughter on Earth.

The first man and woman to have appeared on Earth, the followers of Segbo, produced two children, a boy and a girl. They raised their offspring to honor and worship the gods of the sky in the received manner. After seven years, the first parents also returned to the sky but their children remained on Earth and populated the lands of Dahomey with faithful followers of Mawu-Lisa and the other deities of the Fon.

Invariably a symbol of wise chieftainship, the elephant was once more widely distributed in Africa than today, with man its only predator and the pygmies being particularly expert in hunting it. Prehistoric rock art from what is now South Africa, most probably the ancient work of San people.

The Duality of Twinship

Twins in African tradition are usually fraternal rather than identical, and often of opposing genders. In many cultures twin children were viewed with awe as bringers either of great happiness or of misfortune. Among the Ngbandi people of Central Africa, twins were believed to be snakes and so a manifestation of the tribe's *toro* or supreme god, the serpent. A twin who killed a snake believed he or she had killed a sibling—even if the other twin was evidently still alive—and had to mourn to avert illness or catastrophe.

The Yoruba of Nigeria traditionally believed that twins—or *ibejis*—had their own *orisha* or protective deity named Ibeji, and parents treated twins very kindly in order to prevent Ibeji growing angry and punishing the family (see box opposite). The Yoruba particularly associated twins with *abikus* or souls who die in childhood but keep returning by being born again and again to the same parents.

A Yoruba tale describes how the first twins were sent by angry monkeys to punish a farmer in the town of Ishokun who had driven them from his fields when they came to steal his crops. He was prosperous and had many wives. When one of them became pregnant, a traveling seer warned him that the monkeys were furious and might send an *abiku* to torment him. He advised the farmer to stop fighting the monkeys, but the farmer paid no attention. Two monkeys became *abikus* and were born to the farmer's wife. They were the first twins ever seen among the Yoruba. Some people thought it a good omen of fruitfulness, but others had noticed that female monkeys often bore twins and thought that it augured evil.

The twins soon died, but the next time the farmer's wife gave birth they returned. Again they died, but once more they came back, for they were *abikus*. Eventually a diviner advised that the monkeys be allowed to come and go freely and to feed on the crops. Even so the farmer's wife bore twins again. He returned to the diviner, who explained that these babies were not *abikus*. He taught the man to indulge the twins and the children brought him prosperity.

Yoruba *ibeji* figures carved to placate the powerful spirit of the dead child and to honor and enhance the mother's fertility.

Prosperity or Disaster

Twins faced an unpredictable reception in Africa, for different peoples had strikingly dissimilar responses to their birth. The Yoruba welcomed them as having the capacity to bring prosperity to their family, but other cultures feared them as malign.

Among the Yoruba, the first-born of a pair of twins was often considered to be the younger of the two, sent ahead by his or her elder sibling to test the waters of life. The first-born might be named Taiyewo ("Come to Try Life") and the second Kehinde ("Come Last").

However, in other West African traditions twins were a sign of ill omen. At one time the peoples of eastern Nigeria would send twins back to their maker by leaving them out in pots in the forest. Far to the south in Mozambique, the Thonga devised rituals to prevent evil following the birth of twins: mother and children were sent to dwell on the fringe of the village and the twins, even when grown, were never entirely integrated into tribal life. But the Thonga also saw the twins as having special powers, for they called them "children of the sky" and when a storm threatened, the people would ask them to use their influence to drive it away.

In some places mothers of twins were ritually powerful people; elsewhere they were considered a danger. Wooden Baga figure with twin children.

Divine Twins

Twin beings played a central role in the religious mythology of the Fon people. The chief Fon deity was the twin-faced being named Mawu-Lisa: the female part, Mawu, associated with the moon; and the male one, Lisa, linked to the sun. Mawu-Lisa, male and female, swelled with child: her first-born were twins—a male Da Zodji, and a female named Nyohwe Ananu—who were among the chief Earth deities. She later gave birth to all the great gods of the Fon pantheon. Next to emerge was the thunder god Sogbo or So, who like his mother-father was an androgynous man-woman. More twins followed: Agbe, male, and Naete, female, who became deities of the sea. The hunting god Age was born fourth and Gu, god of war and iron, was born fifth. Born sixth was Djo, the air. Seventh and last to issue from Mawu-Lisa was Legba, whose role was trickster, interpreter, and messenger (see pages 104–107). In some accounts, however, all these seven deities were born as male-female twins.

The Dogon of Mali held that after the great god Amma had made the Earth and heavens (see page 36) he was overcome with loneliness and sought sexual congress with Earth. The first child of the union was a crafty and untrustworthy jackal. But the second time Amma united with the Earth, his partner gave issue to the Nummo, twin spirits with human heads and torsos and serpents' tails. The divine twins gave form to Amma's vital quality, the creative motion that sustains the universe and can be found in light and in water. To each child born on Earth, the Nummo spirits give twin souls, one male and one female: all humans are both female and male until they are initiated into adulthood, when they become fully male or wholly female.

43

The Origin of Cattle

Pastoralist peoples such as the Masai of East Africa or the Fulani of West Africa owed their survival and prosperity to the broad-backed cattle that they herded. The economic and cultural importance of these beasts inspired a rich mythology about their origin.

The Masai were pastoral nomads who from the fourteenth century onward migrated into East Africa from the north, displacing and subjugating local peoples and seizing their herds. One of their principal myths validates this control of the herds, explaining why neighboring peoples such as the Dorobo were not herdsmen but hunters.

At one time, say the Masai, a Dorobo herdsman lived on the land with his cow, a serpent, and an elephant. The elephant calved, but when the Dorobo killed both serpent and mother elephant, the calf fled. It met a quick-witted Masai and told him of the Dorobo and his cow. The Masai went to investigate, and once there he heard the god Naiteru-kop summoning the Dorobo to attend him the following morning. At dawn the Masai presented himself in the Dorobo's place. The god told him to build an enclosure and a hut, slaughter and skin a wild calf, hang the meat up in the animal's hide, and then take refuge in the hut, where he should stay and remain unsurprised even if he heard a thundering without. The Masai agreed and did all these things. As he cowered in the hut the sky god dropped a strip of hide from Heaven and sent down a vast herd of cattle.

So many animals crowded into the enclosure that they began to buffet the walls of the hut and the Masai cried out in surprise. Then he went outside and saw the strip of hide disappearing into Heaven. The sky god explained that he would have sent more cattle if the Masai had not shown his alarm. Nevertheless there were plenty in the pen and the Masai began to care for them. The Dorobo had nothing but the weapons of the hunt.

Gift of the Waters

Myths from north Central Africa propose that cattle emerged long ago from rivers or lakes and humans learned to herd and milk them. Some scholars argue that the first cattle to be tamed in prehistoric Africa were the large horned oxen of the Nile

A *tabwa* mask of a water buffalo, from the Kiyunde people. Stories about more domesticated cattle are told among pastoralists; in a version of the Dorobo-Masai story, the Dorobo were outraged at the Masai appropriations and shot down the strap linking Heaven and Earth, causing Naiteru-kop to be driven away.

Valley and say they inspired these tales because they were associated with the river waters.

In a Fulani myth, a princess gave birth to two illegitimate children. An Islamic missionary sent her to the river, telling her that she would meet the father of the infants there; sure enough, a man rose from the water and came to her, so she left her offspring with him and departed.

The man told the children that he would give them wonderful beasts that would provide their livelihood, if they were willing to abandon town life and take up as herdsmen. He instructed the youngsters to walk away from him, calling "Hi! Hi! Hi!" to attract the animals, but told them on no account to look back. The infants did as they were told, except that after a while they grew so curious that they glanced behind them. For one marvelous instant, they glimpsed a never-ending stream of cows emerging from the riverbed, but even as they looked the river turned back to water, leaving them only with the cattle that were already on the bank.

But it was still a good number of animals. Among riverine or lakeside peoples this theme of a steady supply of animals being stemmed as a result of human actions is a recurrent one.

For example, the Nandi people from the northerly shores of Lake Victoria and the Shilluk from the banks of the Nile both told of cattle emerging from primordial waters. The Fulani, too, were historically a waterside people, for they came originally from the region of the River Senegal in West Africa. They traveled eastward as cattle-raising nomads from the thirteenth century onward, and some of them settled in towns, which casts light on the myth's reference to abandoning town life in favor of bush nomadism. Many Fulani people, especially the town-dwellers, converted to Islam (see page 15).

Another Fulani tale reveals how this cattle-rich people kept the animals that the creator had provided them with. A woman had two offspring, a normal boy and a serpent. She cared for both lovingly, building a pen for the snake and providing it with milk. After the parents died, the boy married—but had to keep his serpent-brother hidden from his wife, for she was not to know that her brother-in-law was a snake that drank their valuable milk. But she noticed her husband sneaking away with helpings of milk and her inquisitiveness was such that she found the snake. Afterward, the serpent declared to his brother that he was leaving and commanded the man to follow. That night, under the sparkling stars and caressed by a breeze, they crept out of their village. The serpent led the way to a river and his faithful brother followed. Then the serpent told him to go home; there, he said, the brother would find a calabash (to hold milk or blood) and a rope for a tether—and as long as he kept these he would be rich in cattle.

Life's Staples of Food and Fire

A group of regionally various myths describe how the staple foods of different peoples, such as fruit or grain, were made or found their way to Earth and how early humans discovered, stole, or were shown the secrets of fire.

The lush forests of the Congo basin loom large in the myths of the Ngbandi people, who live along the Oubangui River. One story explains how fruit and vegetables first came to Earth; it tells how the mighty elephant came visiting from its home in the sky and encountered proud Lightning in the forest. Lightning, who in his fury electrifies the heavens before unleashing the wild drumming of thunder, expected a mere elephant to acknowledge his greatness. But the elephant stood his ground, feeling himself to be the equal of any.

The two eyed each other coldly and agreed to have a contest in noise. The elephant went first: he roared so loudly that the trees shook to their roots. But Lightning only looked away. Then came his response: he sent out a tearing crash of thunder that caused widespread devastation, uprooting the trees and making the rivers burst their banks. The terrified elephant fell down dead. Lightning swept contemptuously away to the sky, leaving the elephant on the forest floor. After a while the animal's stomach swelled and finally it burst, releasing the seeds of the vegetables and fruits it had eaten in the forests of the sky. The fertile ground was a welcoming home, and in time many fruits and vegetables flourished wild in the Congo forests.

The First Grains

The Malagasy peoples of Madagascar, who traditionally lived as farmers, told a delicate story of a mother's love to account for the creation of their

The luxuriant forests of Central Africa are home to the pygmy peoples whose supreme being was Kalisia or Lord of the Forest, a figure who protected them as hunters and led game into their traps, provided they had observed the correct rituals.

staple food, rice. The mother took her child with her one day when she went to work in the fields by a river and the girl's bright eyes were attracted by a springing grasshopper. The mother caught the grasshopper and gave it to her daughter to play with, but when the end of the day came the child could not find the insect and wailed with distress.

She never recovered from the disappointment for she soon sickened and died. The mother was beyond comfort and her cries of anguish reached the creator in Heaven. God was deeply affected by the strength of the mother's love and spoke to the woman, telling her to bury her child's body in a marsh. She returned faithfully to tend the grave and in time she found grains there, which God told her to pound, cook, and then eat. In this way, an unfortunate mother grew the first crop of rice on the island of Madagascar.

In Zambia the Ila told a morality tale of how their ancestors were wasteful with the first crops and thus condemned humanity to go hungry from time to time. When these first Zambians came down from Heaven, the creator gave them grain to plant. They reaped a magnificent harvest and feasted long and late but in their foolishness they threw the surplus on the fire. Dearth followed plenty, the new crops failed, and the people grew hungry. When they appealed to the creator, however, he told them that because they had failed to replant seeds and wasted their resources they now had to make do with fruits and roots.

A *damba* headdress from the Baga people of Guinea, early 20th century. The cloaked figure of a woman who has borne children, it served to promote human and agricultural fertility.

Fire from on High

The Ila also told how a common insect named the mason wasp brought fire down from Heaven. The wasp is not choosy as to where it builds its mud nests, and has a particular fondness for fireplaces, which must explain its role in this origin myth. In bad weather when the sun became a stranger to the Earth, cold troubled the animals, birds, and insects. When they gathered to discuss the matter, the mason wasp volunteered to scale the sheer wall of the sky in order to approach the creator and ask for fire. Then the crow, fish-eagle, and vulture said they would go with her.

All four set off, but one by one the wasp's companions failed and their bones fell to the ground: first the vulture, then the fish-eagle, and finally the crow. Undaunted, the wasp continued on her way. She could not make it to the very top of Heaven, but the creator came down to speak to her. He was happy to reward her bravery by allowing her to return to Earth with the priceless gift of fire.

The pygmies of the Central African forests said that one of their hunters brought back fire from the encampment where the creator himself lived. The hunter had chanced on the encampment when the creator's mother, who was warming herself by the flames, had fallen asleep; the hunter stole the fire, but the old woman grew cold, woke, and called her son, who caught the pygmy and retrieved the fire. The pygmy brought news of his great discovery home; another hunter tried to steal the fire but failed. Then a third hunter plucked some feathers from a bird and with a courageous leap set out on the wing in search of the fire. He found and took the flame and, because he could fly wherever the creator chased him, escaped. Finally the creator accepted that he had met his match and allowed the pygmy to keep the fire. But upon returning to his camp, the creator found his mother was lifeless with cold and in that instant laid the curse of death on people.

47

Ancient Serpent Beings

Sometimes seen as the first and proudest of all creatures, the serpent was associated with royal power. In many traditions it had divine status as creator god or supreme being, considered ancient partly because of its ability to shed its skin and become young again.

The Fon of Dahomey said the snake was so old that it existed even before the Earth was made. As the divine male serpent Aido-Hwedo, he served the great creator Mawu. She rode in his mouth, and wherever she desired to go Aido-Hwedo took her. Her creation took a serpentine form, which explains why the Earth is not flat and plain but has winding rivers, deep valleys, and steep slopes.

From time to time Mawu and Aido-Hwedo rested, and then the serpent's excrement piled up in vast mounds that became the sheer-sided peaks of mountain ranges. This waste contained mineral riches within it, and because the mountain rocks have solidified from it they hide great wealth in their depths that people have learned to dig out. Mawu's creation took the shape of a vast calabash, split in two: the lower half contained waters on which the Earth floated while the top half was wide sky, home of the life-giving rains and of light (see page 35).

Mawu understood that the Earth was too heavy, for it was filled with an abundance of mountains, forests, herds of elephants, and beasts of prey. She knew that it needed something to support it. Then in her wisdom Mawu told Aido-Hwedo to lay himself down on the wide waters in a perfect circle with his tail in his mouth (subsequently an African symbol of eternity). On top she set the Earth and the serpent prevents it sinking. In other versions Aido-Hwedo lies around the horizon, binding the top and bottom halves of the calabash.

In some accounts, Mawu made the waters especially for Aido-Hwedo in order to keep him cool—he is known to dislike heat and so lies in the sea. Sometimes he shifts and then the Earth shudders in an earthquake. In one version Aido-Hwedo created rivers and streams: when Mawu first made the Earth there was no running water, only pools, but Aido-Hwedo led the first streams and rivers in a winding path across the land.

Bronze python's head from the West African kingdom of Benin where the cosmic serpent was seen as a divine, creative force. Living both in the trees and under the ground, the python was believed to act as a messenger of the god Olukun and was addressed respectfully as "our king."

Ancestral Snake

The Ngbandi of northern Congo also believed that the snake was the oldest of all the animals. They revered the serpent as their supreme god and the spirit of their tribe. The Ngbandi held the leopard in awe, and said that after death the tribal chief's soul took on the body of a leopard; but the snake had primacy even over this princely animal. The snake's mother was the dragonfly. Twins were viewed as human representations of the divine snake (see page 42).

In a number of African cultures the serpent was associated with the primeval ancestor who founded the tribe or led it to its homeland. The Venda took part in the great southward migration of Bantu-speaking peoples and by the seventeenth century had reached parts of what is now Zimbabwe. They tell a story in which the tribe's founders sprang from a snake's body. In ancient days, they say, a serpent named Tharu stirred on a mountainside that had been baked bone dry by the sun. He divided into two halves, Thoho ("The Head") and Tshamutshila ("The Tail"), who went their separate ways in search of food.

Tshamutshila settled in a fertile country and became a man. He herded good cattle, raised excellent crops, married fine-boned women of proud bearing, and gave issue to a magnificent tribe of children: the Venda. He took the name Ramabulana. His brother Thoho ended up in a dusty land where no crops would grow; he too became a man, but he could not settle and had to earn his food as a minstrel.

One day Thoho came to the Venda city where Ramabulana ruled. At the gates he played and

sang, managing to attract a large crowd. Even Ramabulana's wives went to watch and they returned in a state of high excitement, clamoring for their husband to venture out and be entertained. Now Ramabulana knew the identity of the minstrel and he feared to meet him—in case, when they stood close, they should once again become a single serpent. But his wives insisted so loudly that he went to see Thoho.

It was precisely as the king had feared. The moment Ramabulana saw his brother he fell to the ground, once again a slithering python. Thoho also reverted to serpent form and the two were fused as of old in the body of the primeval python Tharu. As the Venda people looked on in horror the great snake slipped away into the landscape, to be seen no more. Tshamutshila-Ramabulana's sons quarreled over the kingship and, with their clans, each went their separate ways as part of the great migration of Venda.

The Kom, whose lands are near Bamenda in northwest Cameroon, also told of an ancestor's transformation into a serpent prior to a migration. After a conflict with Fon tribesmen, the Kom chief told his kinsmen to follow the track of a python when it should appear. Then he took his own life. Sure enough, a python's track appeared—and it led the Kom ancestors to the site of their royal capital. As well as being associated with mythical tribal ancestors, snakes feature in many stories as kingmakers; when they are seen fawning on a warrior or hunter, it is a sure sign that the individual has been fated for greatness.

SCARS OF ANCESTRY

The creation of decorative scarring patterns is an ancient African custom, probably dating back to Neolithic times. There is even a rock painting in the Sahara, at Tassili N'Ajjer, of a horned goddess (c.7000 BCE) with signs of scars on her breasts, belly, thighs, shoulders, and calves. Far from being considered mutilation, cicatrice or scarification was undertaken willingly for a variety of reasons: to provide permanent beautification; to offer a visible sign of collective affiliation or individual identity; to indicate social status; to eroticize the body and signal sexual attraction or assertiveness; to produce sensual pleasure; to mark a rite of passage; or to undergo enhancing sensations which enabled communion with ancestral spirits and emphasized spiritual and cosmological relationships in the process. Meanings differed; for the Tiv of Nigeria, for example, the committment required to undergo it was testament of one's unselfishness; while for the Baule of the Ivory Coast, deliberate body-scarring was the inscribing of cultural order on nature—an unadorned body thus denoted the crude and uncivilized.

Left: The peoples of the Congo, notably Luba and Tabwa, used many types of symmetrical patterns and even filed their teeth in imitation of the fish upon which they depended. Northern Congo, c.1900.

Left: Spirit-world spouse or *blolo bla* of the Baule. Men and women of this clanless people wore the same scars. *Kanga* lines on the mouth guarded against disease and misfortune.

Right: Wooden *lipiko* mask from the Makonde of Mozambique. Decorated with real hair, it was worn in male circumcision rite dances and may have caricatured a haughty convert to Islam.

Above: Scarring is often associated with growing fertility. In early adolescence girls receive their first body scars, gaining more complex ones as they mature and when they give birth. Male lovers find some highly erogenous. Nuer girl, Sudan.

Above: For many Africans body marks were related to female sexuality. For example, the Tiv word for "belly design" also meant "sexual lust." In Nigeria, women with raised scars were considered to be more likely to bear lots of children. Fulani woman, Nigeria.

Right: This Wongo cup represents a high-status female with elaborate scarification patterning. As founders of dynasties, women were associated with life, death, and renewal: the navel and breasts were linked to fecundity. The red of the camwood symbolized transition.

AN ORDERED WORLD

Just as people in Africa wished to know how humankind had been created and the land and sea had come into being, so they also sought explanations of why the world they lived in was the way it was. Why did everyone have to die? How was it that diviners could foretell the future? What gave the fearsome sorcerers and witches their power? How did the different species of animal get their special characteristics? What caused men and women to be assigned their respective social roles?

In the absence of books to resolve these and myriad other puzzles, people turned to the storytellers, who claimed for their solutions the authority of ancestral knowledge. They could not quote chapter and verse on the written page as proof of what they said; instead they appealed to tradition to validate their claims. The stories, they maintained, had been passed down by word of mouth from generation to generation since time immemorial. Their very antiquity meant that they must be true.

In fact it is almost impossible now to estimate how old most of the tales are, or even to date the social customs and institutions that they explain. The first written collections were made only over the past two centuries, yet even in that comparatively short time the myths have changed. The stories told today are in many respects markedly different from those recounted at the close of the nineteenth century.

For the very absence of a literary tradition gives the myths an unusual fluidity. While quoting tradition as a sanction, every individual storyteller is free to add or subtract details from the tale they are telling as their art requires. They can adapt their narratives to the desires and expectations of their audience in a way that people working with the written word seldom can.

Such flexibility is particularly important when it comes to explaining the ways of the living world, for social customs and traditions are themselves constantly in flux. That mutability goes a long way to explaining the richness of Africa's myths on social themes. For although the eternal questions that people pose may themselves stay more or less the same over time, the answers vary constantly, not just from country to country or culture to culture but also from generation to generation.

Above: Arrayed with protective charms used in religious rites, this magic figure of wood and metal wears a square-brimmed hat often associated with hunter figurines and bush spirits. Fon, Guinea coast, 19th century.

Opposite: Real leopards kept in the palace at Benin were paraded in public on important occasions, reflecting the animal's status as a royal symbol and also evoking its supernatural power. Nineteenth-century carved ivory leopard, inlaid with bronze, with a coral necklace as a mark of ritual allegiance.

53

The Coming of Death

In most African mythologies, death was not part of the original creation. A wealth of stories set out to explain how it first came into the world, some of them suggesting an accidental origin and others an intention to punish.

One of the best-known stories among the Bantu-speakers of the south uses a tortoise-and-hare motif to explain death's arrival—only in this case the hare wins. The tale tells how the Supreme Being, having created the first people, sent a chameleon to give them the good news that they would live forever. He could hardly have chosen a worse messenger. The reptile—traditionally a creature of ill omen—plodded off at a snail's pace, and was constantly distracted along the way by the urge to feed and rest. Before it had got halfway, the deity had second thoughts and decided that people must die. He entrusted this pronouncement to a speedy gecko. The lizard scurried off busily and in next to no time had overtaken its rival. So the bad news reached people first, and as no divine edict could ever be contradicted, death has been the fate of all living things ever since.

While the Bantu story makes death's coming almost accidental, other traditions saw it as the result of a curse or the breaking of a taboo. For the Luyia, it was the fault of an unloving parent. In the first times, they claimed, the dead came back to life again after four days. But one mother refused to take her deceased son back into her home, saying that he was dead and should stay that way. Reluctantly he left the land of living, but in doing so he cursed those he left behind, and from that time forth no one has come back from the land of the dead.

Protective bronze amulet with double-headed snake motif. Lobi people, Burkina Faso.

The tales in which death enters the world through a taboo sometimes unconsciously parallel well-known Western myths. For example, there are echoes of Pandora's box in the story told by the Lamba of Zambia, in which God sends the seeds of essential crops and plants to humankind in small bundles, giving strict instructions to his messengers to deliver them unopened. But curiosity gets the better of the couriers and they untie the packages to see what is inside, thereby spreading not the gift of life but death itself over the world.

In the same way, a story told of the Baganda hero Kintu hints at a motif known in the West from the Greek myth of Orpheus and Eurydice, as well as from the tale of Lot's wife in the Bible. When Kintu was bringing his wife Nambi to Earth from the sky (see pages 120–121), he was given strict instructions to hurry; otherwise, he was told, Nambi's brother Death would come with them. The couple were given the plants, fowls, and domestic animals they needed to set up house and set out on their descent. But halfway down Nambi realized she had forgotten to bring grain to feed the chickens, and insisted on going back for it. The delay proved fatal, permitting Death to catch up with them and thereby introducing mortality into the world.

In other traditions, people asked for death to come. Sometimes they did so to escape the grim reality of aging, as in the Dogon story of the first ancestor who grew so old that

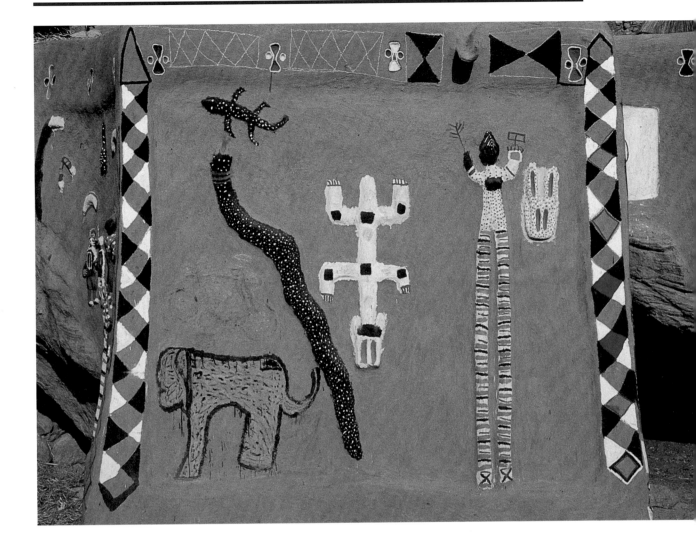

Important symbols adorn a wall painting in a Dogon escarpment settlement. The tribe was led there, the people believe, by a snake; the other figures shown are all intended to influence the spirit world that surrounds everyday life.

he could no longer move even to relieve his bowels or bladder. Faced by the miseries of double incontinence, he begged the god who had made him to let him die, and his request was granted. For the Nuer of Sudan, death was the solution to overpopulation. Seeing the world filling up with people, their ancestors implored God to let some die to make room for fresh generations, and he reluctantly agreed.

Even so, death was at best a necessary evil, and people envied a creature like the snake that could seemingly evade it by sloughing off its old skin. Sierra Leone's Kono claimed that God had meant people to be able to renew themselves in the

same way, but he gave the bundle containing the new skins to a dog, which failed to guard it properly. While it dallied, a snake stole it and helped itself to the contents. Ever since, humans have died and snakes have shed their skin—but have also been hated by the people they cheated.

An Alur story from the Congo mixes similar concerns with a theme of shamanistic shapeshifting. It tells of a primeval ancestor who lived with

55

her granddaughter in the forest. She had the power to renew herself by shedding her skin, but on pain of death had to do so in private. But one day the little girl rushed in to tell her a cooking pot was boiling over and found her with her skin off. This rude interruption cost the life not only of the old woman, who died as a result, but also all her descendants, for she could not pass on the secret of rejuvenation as had been intended.

Some traditions maintain that initially death was voluntary, and those who chose to die could do so by climbing up a rope or chain hanging from the sky. A tale told by the Ronga of Mozambique

described what happened when a childless girl decided to ascend it. At the top she found a ruined village inhabited by a single old woman. The crone directed her further on, telling her that if she felt an ant in her ear she should take care not to kill it but instead listen to the advice it gave her. The girl obeyed, and was directed by the insect to

Mukenge spirit masks underlined the liaison between human rulers and the forces of nature by representing royal ancestors as elephants. The masks were placed on the deceased ruler's mannequin upon his death. The trunk and tusks are clearly visible on this late 19th-century Ngeende example from Congo.

another village inhabited by shining beings who asked her why she had come. When she told them that she wanted a baby, they gave her a choice of several infants, and her tiny friend steered her to the one she was foreordained to have. Then she was given many rich presents and sent with the child back to the land of the living.

Seeing her success, her unpleasant sister tried to emulate it, but with disastrous results. She was rude to the old woman, scorned the ant's advice, and chose the wrong baby. No sooner had she done so than she was struck down dead by a clap of thunder, and her bones fell back to earth, landing on her old home.

Some legends personify Death, not always in an unsympathetic light. A story of the Mbundu of Angola tells of a man's grief when, on returning from a journey, he found that the grim reaper had come for his beloved younger brother. In his rage he vowed revenge, and had a trap made by a skilled blacksmith. He set it in the bush outside his village, and before long found that he had caught Death himself. When he reproached the dread lord, Death replied that he was not to blame; it was humans who were responsible for most fatalities, whether their own or other people's.

To prove the point he invited the young man to the Land of the Dead. There the mortal watched as the newly dead arrived and found it was just as his host had claimed; some had been killed by the sorcery of envious neighbors, others had died as a result of their own vices and follies. Then he was taken to see his brother, who turned down the chance of returning to the world of the living, saying he was quite happy to stay where he was.

One point that almost all the stories agree on is that Death follows his own agenda. That point is forcibly made in a Yoruba legend about a man who

Prestige drinking vessel made from wood and brass in the form of a human head. Kuba-Bushoong, Congo, 19th century.

went to look for Death. It tells of a rich merchant, Aiye-Gbege, who lost his wealth and with it his wives and servants, who all deserted him. Reduced to begging, he resolved to die. But when he went in search of Death, he could not find him. Everyone he asked told him that it was Death's job to do the looking, not his.

But at last he met an old man who said that, while Death himself was not to be found, he could at least speak to his agent, a man named Ayo. With the man's help he managed to track down Ayo and told him his problem. Ayo promised to pass on the message to his master. Meanwhile, to lessen Aiye-Gbege's suffering, he provided him with fine clothes, gold, and a horse to carry him home.

The gifts transformed Aiye-Gbege's life. When he got back to his native town, word of his changed condition quickly spread. All his long-lost friends reappeared, as did his wives and servants. Soon his fortunes were as good as they had ever been, and he regained the will to live.

A year after his return, he decided to hold a feast to celebrate his good luck. He invited half the town, and there was much dancing and drinking of palm wine. No one enjoyed themselves more than Aiye-Gbege, who mounted his steed and set it prancing and rearing among the guests. But he was drunk and lost his seat, striking his head as he fell. The blow knocked him cold.

When he came to, all the revelers had gone. But he was not alone. Death stood before him. Vainly Aiye-Gbege protested that he no longer wanted to die. The stranger cut him short by pointing out curtly, "When you were poor, you at least had the gift of life. Happiness has killed you." And then Death, who waits for no man, took Aiye-Gbege.

Living in Terror of Witches

Even today, belief in witchcraft is widespread in Africa. Fear of its practitioners is also prevalent, for African witches, even more than their Western counterparts, are always malevolent, seeking to kill their victims by secretly consuming their souls.

African concepts of witchcraft draw on the idea that sickness and death are not necessarily natural. Often they may be caused by the intervention of evil spirits—and like as not these will be under the control of a malign individual.

Such people are not always conscious of their powers. Some may simply be born with the evil eye, causing misery around them with no deliberate intent to do harm. Among their ranks are East Africa's *kisirani*, hapless individuals whose mere presence in a room is enough to make valuables lose themselves and send treasured pots tumbling.

An Urge for Evil

More serious misfortunes are likely to be blamed on intentional witchcraft or sorcery, which are used to explain all kinds of tragedy, in particular unexpected deaths. Belief in them stirs many primal fears, for witchcraft is very hard for ordinary people to detect except by its terrible results.

Witches, who may be male as well as female, show no obvious exterior sign of their condition. On the surface they may be likeable and even charming people, only revealing their true nature in private, usually under cover of night. Many stories make the point that they may be found close to home: as neighbors, in-laws, or even in one's own family.

Yet underneath their seemingly harmless exterior, witches are entirely evil, driven by an irresistible urge to consume the spiritual strength of their victims—to "eat their soul," as the saying goes. Sometimes they use poison to achieve their ends, but more often the damage is done spiritually. By obtaining objects intimately connected with the targeted individual—such as hairs, nail clippings, or even excreta—they can find a pathway into his or her psyche and transmit a pathogen invisible to the eye of all but a skilled witch doctor. The affected person will sicken and die for no apparent reason.

Sorcerers and Zombie Slaves

There is no clear line between witchcraft and sorcery, except that sorcerers tend to work on their own. Some can shift shape, taking on the form of birds or animals. Often it is only the soul of the

An array of monkey skulls embedded in a hut wall decorates the home of a "spirit master," a curer of witches, who can control the energies released by the process of death itself. Witches themselves live in grave danger from fellow humans who fear them. Dogon, Mali.

sorcerer that inhabits these animal familiars, while his body may be elsewhere altogether. There are many stories of people dying in their beds at the exact moment that a hunter killed the owl, bat, snake, hyena, or crocodile sheltering their spirit.

More alarmingly still, some sorcerers dig up dead bodies and bring them back to a terrible half-life as zombies: the word itself comes from the Kongo term for an object of spiritual power (see also page 136). The Zulu of South Africa call these living dead *umkovu* and say that they can only mumble inarticulately, for their tongues are slit to prevent them from talking. The resuscitated corpses then become their animator's slaves.

One tale from Natal describes how a man who had lost his brother to an unexplained illness became convinced that he had fallen victim to sorcery, and set out to find the person responsible. He wandered far and wide, asking everyone he met if they knew anyone who could have caused the young man's death. Eventually he met someone who, although too afraid to speak, pointed him in the direction of nearby hills. There he found his brother at last. He was one of a ghostly host of laborers, all silently hoeing the extensive fields of a sorcerer who had grown rich by exercising his necromantic powers. The seeker led his brother home, but he had lost the power of

A Bellyful of Evil

In many parts of Africa, the stomach is the seat of evil. For the Ngbandi of the northern Congo the spirits that enter it are called li *and the people they possess are* li-men.

Li-men behave like other African witches, doing harm to their victims by obtaining nail clippings or pieces of their clothing. They walk by night, and anyone whose door they knock on is sure to waste away and die in a few days. They are cannibals and dig up corpses to eat the flesh. Some steal children in order to kill and consume them.

Yet by day these terrible creatures are indistinguishable from their neighbors. The only way to identify them is after death, when witchfinders known as "belly-cutters" may be summoned to perform an autopsy. Cutting open the corpse, they will carefully examine the stomach and intestines. If they find a tumor, they will declare it to be the abode of the *li* and will take care to see that it is removed far from the village. As for the dead man's relatives, they will become objects of general suspicion, for the *li* are known to haunt whole families.

A carrier of magic from the land of the spirits, this *nkisi* *nkondi* **was collected in Congo before 1878. The many nails provide protection from spirit forces regulating the world.**

59

speech and died soon after. His corpse, which had previously remained limp, now stiffened in the normal way, indicating that he was truly dead.

Coven of the Cannibals

Unlike sorcerers, witches assemble in covens to eat the flesh of corpses; each member is expected to provide a body in turn, and these are often the remains of murdered relatives or neighbors. A sense of the terror they inspire comes through strongly in a tale of the Kongo people, who inhabit the lower reaches of the Congo River. This describes how a young woman named Malemba went to visit her boyfriend, little knowing that he was really a witch. She slipped into his hut surreptitiously at twilight, so that the neighbors would not see, then sat quietly in the darkness waiting for him to return.

When he did so, he failed to notice her. Instead, he took down a basket of food left for him by other members of the coven, and Malemba was horrified to see him pick out and eat a human finger. Her disgust turned to terror when he muttered curses at his fellow witches for leaving him such slim pickings, and promised that they would get no better from him—when the time came for him to kill Malemba.

At that point he lit a torch and saw his intended victim. Malemba tried hard to act as though she had heard nothing, but she could tell that he was not convinced. Muttering some excuse he soon left the hut, and Malemba realized that he must have gone to fetch the rest of the coven.

Panic-stricken, she fled back toward her own village. But the witches took down a fetish—a wooden carving imbued with magical power.

It twisted like a live thing in their hands, seeking the girl as a predator scents its prey. Soon it was pointing out the path that she had taken, and the six members of the coven were running at full pelt in pursuit of their victim.

The girl took refuge in her mother's garden, hiding under a pile of refuse. Her pursuers soon neared and would have found her had an antelope—perhaps a good spirit in disguise—not suddenly leaped out of the undergrowth and thrown the fetish off her track. Confused in the nightime darkness, the men ran off after the beast. They soon came back, but just as they arrived dawn broke, forcing them to hurry off back to their own village.

The girl was found by her mother more dead than alive. She was able to tell her parents what had happened, but remained desperately weak through the day. The final straw came at dusk that evening when the six witches came to the hut, seemingly on a harmless social visit. The sight of them was more than the sick girl could bear, and she finally passed away.

Her parents saw that her death did not go unpunished. They accused her boyfriend and his five accomplices before the chief's council. The six were condemned to drink the poison of judgment, fatal to witches although supposedly harmless to the innocent. All perished.

An Enduring Fear

Sorcery and the fear of it is still very much a fact of life in parts of the continent, as a recent spate of internationally publicized witch killings in South Africa has made apparent. Often the true

Late 19th-century *tetela* from Congo made of ivory and metal. This figure was made to rest on top of a fetish gourd filled by a diviner with "medicine" to avert misfortune. The protruding objects may have been added as thanksgivings for its power.

The Talking Bowl of Broth

Sorcerers used poison both to kill their victims and to steal their souls. But in one Hausa tale the potion itself spoke up to thwart its maker.

The witch in question had nine mouths on her body, all invisible to ordinary people, and a ravening appetite for evil that led her to seek to kill her own husband and father-in-law. With murder in mind, she gathered noxious herbs from the forest and boiled them up in a broth. But when the two men sat down to eat and uncovered their bowls, a voice from the first warned them, "Cover me up or else you will die." When the same thing happened a second time, the husband became convinced that witchcraft was afoot. Picking up the bowl, he emptied it over his wife's head. Suddenly the nine mouths became visible, and she was revealed as a witch. She ran away from the village and was never seen again.

horror lies less in the accusations that are made—real though the fears they represent may be—than in the violence done to the supposed witches. The annals of African justice are full of stories of people weighed down by grief who, crazed by a presentiment of invisible evil all around them, have committed atrocious acts in an attempt to exorcise the demons haunting them.

So, in 1934, a Luba man whose brother had fallen dangerously ill consulted a diviner who suggested to him that one of his four wives must be responsible—without specifying which one. The man took a knife and stabbed one of the wives to death. When his brother's health failed to improve, he killed another. The same scenario was repeated twice more. Then, with all his wives dead and his wits completely gone, the deluded man dragged his brother from his bed and killed him too, raving that he had no reason to be ill after so many had died for him. Fear of witchcraft can bring about deeds quite as horrible as any ever credited to the witches.

61

Seeking Sanctuary from Shapeshifters

African legend has many tales of living things that, like the werewolves of Europe, could shift shape from human to animal and back again. Most of these menacing creatures were predators who murdered at will; a few, however, were beings of a far gentler disposition who had no wish to inflict harm on anyone.

The best-known tale concerning these were-creatures tells of a particularly choosy girl who turned down all the would-be suitors who sought to woo her, saying that none was the man she was looking for. Her parents almost despaired of seeing her married until one day a handsome stranger happened to pass through the village. She fell in love with him at first sight and lost no time in letting him know of her feelings. Her delighted parents were also taken with the man's courtesy and politeness and were more than content when the two decided to wed.

The one person who was less than impressed was the wife's young brother. He sensed something unusual, even dangerous, about the stranger. Worse, he was convinced that he had once glimpsed a second mouth hidden under the hair at the back of his head—a sure sign that he was a shapeshifting predator, for such creatures invariably kept their fanged jaws concealed, choosing instead to present a pleasant and smiling visage to the world at large.

He did his best to warn his sister and parents, but they would not hear a word said against the

groom. Even so, when the husband invited the wife back to his own village, the boy insisted on accompanying them, despite his sister's efforts to persuade him to stay.

The first night out the three camped in a forest. The husband then went off, saying that he was going to catch some fish for dinner, leaving the other two on their own.

As soon as he had gone, the brother insisted on putting a solid defensive ring of thorn bushes around their sleeping place. It turned out to be labor well spent, for the husband had no sooner left them than he cast off his human skin and took on animal form as a lion. He gathered others around him and the whole pack descended on the camp, their nostrils flaring for human flesh.

The brother and sister spent a terrible night hugging one another by the fire in fear while the yellow-eyed predators paced hungrily around, held back only by the narrow ring of thorns. When dawn broke the beasts stalked off, hungry and frustrated, leaving the couple to collapse into an exhausted sleep.

They were woken soon after when the husband returned, once more in human form and seemingly much concerned for their safety. He pretended that he had come back early the previous evening, but had seen the lions prowling round the camp and had been forced to take refuge to save himself. Not believing a word he said, the brother ran off into the forest, desperately seeking a means of escape.

As he wandered hopelessly, he saw an unexpected sight. It was an *akachekulu*—one of a race of shy, gnome-like creatures renowned among the Bantu peoples for their wisdom. The little being

The Half-People

Abbreviated beings with only one arm, one leg, and half a head and torso are a distinctive element of African mythology.

Tales of these strange half-people are told in many parts of the continent. Sometimes they are described as cannibal monsters, and meeting them means almost certain death. But in other stories they are comparatively benign. Several peoples, for example, have a legend of a being with a body of flesh and bone on one side but on the other of wax. He challenges all he meets to a wrestling contest, and passes on his knowledge of medicinal herbs to those who manage to throw him. In some traditions, those he instructs are forbidden to speak of what they have learned, and may even have to play dumb for a given time before they can take up their normal life again. In Angola, there are tales of an equally kind old half-woman who helps travelers across a dangerous river.

asked him his problem, and he explained the mortal danger confronting him and his sister. The *akachekulu* was not surprised, for he knew all about the were-lion. And he agreed to help the unhappy pair.

First he showed the boy how to cut down a hollow tree trunk and turn it into a drum. Then he cast a spell over it, telling the brother he had only to mimic flight for it to rise up into the air. Excitedly, the boy took the magic drum back to his sister. He arrived just in time to stuff her inside it before her husband came to demand what was going on. Before he could prevent them, the two soared up to treetop level, and even though the man-lion changed back into animal form to race after them the couple were able to fly back to their own village safe from harm. There they were reunited with their parents, and the boy was praised by all his neighbors for his mental acuity in seeing through the predator's wiles.

The world is full of dangers, both natural and supernatural, from which humans take steps to protect themselves. The Somba of Benin say that they found the land inhabited by *yetenkonde*, small people or bush spirits similar to the Bantu's *akachekulu*— probably earlier hunter-gatherers—who granted them the right to settle. This Somba "castle" houses both humans and their animals; it has a pillar and mound in the foreground that serve as an altar for sacrifices to a protective cult.

63

The Diviner's Secret Arts

Across Africa, diviners serve as intermediaries with the spirit world, using a multitude of methods and mystical ploys to decode fate and reveal the will of the gods. A rich lode of legend explains the origins of their calling.

Africa's diviners use their skills to bring back knowledge that would otherwise remain hidden. Amid life's uncertainties they provide their clients with advice on the best course of action, acting as doctors, psychiatrists, and social workers while also benefitting from the mystical aura given off by their supernatural inspiration.

On one calculation, there are more than sixty different divining methods practiced across the continent. These range from astromancy and ornithomancy— telling the future respectively by reading the stars and observing the movements of birds—to various ways of throwing lots, using either sticks, bones, or dice. In

Methods of divination are many and varied, and dozens of different ones are practiced throughout Africa. Mashonaland divining tablets and case, Zimbabwe.

southern parts of Africa, water-filled divining bowls are used; similar ones have been found in the ruins of Great Zimbabwe. Some Bantu peoples simply pour a handful of flour on the floor and study the shape it makes. If it forms a regular cone, the omen is propitious, but signs are bad if it flakes into miniature valleys.

As for the clients, they range from chiefs seeking favorable times for harvesting or celebrating religious rituals to ordinary citizens worried about their health and well-being. Often diviners will be consulted over problems such as infertility or possession by evil spirits, a complaint as common in some areas of Africa as clinical depression is in the West.

They are not the only supernaturally inspired helpers people turn to for advice. Many consult mediums who communicate with spirits while in a trance. Some may be possessed only once or twice in their lifetime, but others claim to be in regular contact with one or more "familiars" that they can identify by name.

In their trances the mediums usually speak a language that ordinary people cannot understand. They are helped by a "doctor" who interprets the message and passes it on to those seeking advice. Sometimes drums or pipes are used to help establish contact with the spirit world.

From Oracles to Ifa

In the past, Africa also had fully fledged oracles, rather like that of Delphi in ancient Greece. One such was located at Aro in eastern Nigeria, in a cave 6.6 ft (2 m) up on a riverbank. Suppliants would stand in the river to hear the priest deliver auguries in a distinctive nasal whine. Sometimes the spirits would accuse an individual of crimes, in which case he would be taken into the cave to be "eaten" by the oracle and would never be seen again. In fact, the victims were smuggled out of another entrance and sold into slavery, a practice that was eventually banned in 1900.

There was a strong tradition of divination in Nigeria. The mythology of the Yoruba gave an important place to Orunmila, the god of the divining system known as *ifa* ("all-embracing"). The eldest son of the great sky god Olodumare, he was not only consulted before the Earth was formed from a watery waste, but also restored it after a primeval flood sent by the sea god Olukun swept away much of the initial creation.

The survivors of the cataclysm were so grateful to him that they tried to persuade him to stay on Earth. He preferred to return to Heaven, but before going decided to make a gesture to conciliate those he was leaving behind. He chose selected individuals and gave them knowledge of *ifa*, which was ever afterward sacred to him. The first practitioners passed the secret on to the next generation, and it has been transmitted in similar fashion to the present day.

The *ifa* system involves casting palm nuts in multiples of four and using the results to create patterns in sand on a divining board. By practicing it, devotees can share the knowledge of Orunmila, conceived of as a wise, sober figure who is privy

The Tortoise's Revenge

According to the mythology of the Fon people, Tortoise served as the diviner for the animal race—and he could prove a bitter enemy to anyone who failed to show him due respect.

There was no love lost between Monkey and Tortoise, the one so agile and the other so slow. So when, during a famine, Monkey found a field of grain ready for harvesting, the last thing he would normally have done was go to Tortoise for assistance. But each time he tried to get at the crop, he was driven away by the farmer. Eventually he decided that he would never succeed without the Tortoise's magic, and so went to consult the diviner.

At first Tortoise was unwilling to help, saying that Monkey would run off and give him nothing in return. And when he was finally persuaded, his fears proved well founded. He starved while Monkey stuffed himself. But then Leopard came along, seeking a cure for a sick cub.

It was just the break Tortoise needed to get his revenge. He told Leopard that there was only one cure for the ailment: a monkey's head and tail. Then he pointed out that the ingredients were at hand, indicating Monkey in the nearby field.

Thus Monkey came to an untimely end. Leopard got the head and tail he needed, leaving the torso to feed the hungry Tortoise. And, said the Fon with their own diviners no doubt in mind, Tortoise also made sure he received the large fee he always charged for his services.

to the secrets of the supreme sky god himself. To counterbalance his gravity, the myths pair him off with Eshu, a trickster spirit representing cosmic disruption. Through their unlikely friendship, the forces of order and anarchy go hand in hand.

Naturally enough, there is a myth to explain how this unlikely pairing came about. As the tale has it, Orunmila's knowledge of the future was the envy of all the *orishas* or lesser gods. In particular, they hankered after the bag in which he carried his divining equipment. Orunmila could not help noticing their covetousness, and came up with a plan to find out just how loyal his friends really were.

To put it into practice, he got his wife to spread the word that he had died, then hid out of sight to see how the other *orishas* took the news. As he had feared, the very first to console the widow had hardly finished expressing his sorrow before mentioning that the dead man had promised him his divining board as a last bequest. The next offered to relieve her of the bag as a favor; the third claimed it in lieu of a fictitious undischarged debt.

Of all the gods, only one did not try to get his hands on the precious bag and that was Eshu, who simply came to express his sympathy without any ulterior motive. Even when Orunmila's wife asked if he had not been promised it, Eshu would have none of it, instead owning up to a debt that he had owed Orunmila. At that point the god stepped out and clasped Eshu to him, saying he was his only true friend. And from that time on it became common for Yoruba to say of boon companions that they were "as close as Eshu and Orunmila."

An *ifa* divination tray used for the oracular rituals during which the will of the gods is announced and the person's prayers are relayed. Palm nuts are shaken in the bowl to reveal the prediction. Yoruba, 19th century.

Eshu and the Oba

Even so, Eshu was a difficult companion at the best of times, as the story of Orunmila's visit to the town of Owo made clear. Usually so organized, the god made the mistake of not getting a clear assurance from his divining kit that the trip would be auspicious. As things turned out, Eshu's penchant for practical jokes almost turned it into a disaster. For the trickster put a pile of kola fruits by the roadside and the god, weary from the journey, could not resist the temptation of eating one. No sooner had he put the fruit to his mouth than a farmer appeared, just as Eshu intended, wanting to know why he had stolen his produce. Orunmila protested his innocence to no avail. The angry farmer tried to wrest the fruit away from the god, and in the ensuing violent tussle the palm of Orunmila's hand was slashed by the farmer's bush knife.

When Orunmila finally reached the city, it was to find that the farmer had formally accused him, before the authorities, of theft. Things looked bad, for the farmer was citing the cut on his hand as proof that Orunmila was the robber.

Eshu now realized that his joke was getting out of control. So the night before Orunmila was summoned before the city's *oba* or ruler, he went around the city cutting the hand of every citizen, including the *oba* himself, as they slept. Then, when Orunmila appeared before the *oba* the next day and was asked to open his palm, Eshu—acting as his advocate—insisted that everyone else in the court should do the same. Seeing slashed palms on all sides, the *oba* declared that Orunmila should be released from captivity and paid compensation. Suddenly the god found himself overwhelmed with gifts of fruit, not to mention chickens, goats, and palm wine. Even so, it was a long time before he chose to go traveling with Eshu again.

Over the centuries, the Yoruba divining system acquired such prestige that it was adopted by neighboring peoples, who included the Fon of the Dahomey kingdom. The Fon believed that every individual had a fate that was written down at the time of their creation. Knowledge of this destiny could be obtained through the divining system they called simply *fa*. And once an individual's *fa* had been expounded, he was expected to keep the sand, mixed with certain secret magical substances, in a small cloth bag, which became his own personal sacred relic linking him to the god who presided over his destiny.

Voice of the Spirits

In parts of Africa, just as in Australia and New Guinea, the bull-roarer was sometimes said to be the voice of the spirits.

Noise-making figures atop a Yoruba Oro Society dance mask, Nigeria.

A tapered oval of stone or wood, the bull-roarer produces an eerie wailing when whirled overhead on a length of cord. In many African societies, only initiates were allowed to learn its secret, for it was used in ceremonies to mimic the voice of gods or spirits.

A Yoruba story about its first appearance probably contains more than a grain of historical truth. It describes how, at a time of high infant mortality, men called *babalaawo*—initiates in *ifa* divination—told their fellows that they must worship a new god if they wished to save their children. This was Oro, the spirit of the bull-roarer, whose effigy the *babalaawo* themselves had fashioned. They told the people to dance and sing so that Oro would talk, appealing on their behalf to the Supreme God not to take the children.

The people did as they were told and the children stopped dying. But one day their king insisted that his wives should be present when Oro sang.

That day the fetish was silent. When the king asked the *babalaawo* for the reason, they explained that it was against the rules for women to hear Oro's cry. So the women went home and Oro once more wailed for the celebrants. The story ends matter-of-factly, "Hence it is from that day Oro is not made in the presence of women."

67

Brotherhoods of the Initiates

Secret societies and hereditary priesthoods are a distinctive feature of African life, particularly in the west of the continent. There is a rich mythology to explain the origins of these politically influential, invariably single-sex, organizations.

Secret societies are a particularly strong phenomenon on West Africa's Guinea coast and in the Congo basin, but are unknown in the eastern and southern parts of the continent. They are usually men-only organizations and they exercise real political power; in some countries anyone wishing to hold a position of authority almost has to be a member, and rulers can be deposed if they clash with the societies. For that reason, they have been banned in some areas such as Dahomey and among the Ashanti of Ghana.

In many cases "secret" is something of a misnomer, as the members participate in impressive public rituals, usually wearing masks. These extravagant spectacles can conceal the fact that the societies also have a significant social role, sometimes even providing education for their members. They also play an important role in regulating conduct. The Leopard Societies of the Congo regularly punish those who offend against accepted codes of behavior, coming to their homes at night and taking them away to suffer humiliation or worse. Yet all seek supernatural sanction for their activities; members don masks to participate in spirit-summoning rituals and call on gods and ancestors to explain and justify their existence.

One of the best-known groups is the Poro Society, based among the Mende of Sierra Leone but also widespread in neighboring Liberia; a parallel organization known as the Sande exists for women. Highly hierarchical, the Poro numbers many of the nation's highest-ranking officials among its members. As well as initiating its recruits into manhood, the society also concerns itself with their future careers, providing training in crafts.

The central focus of the society was and remains the preparation of adolescent boys to take their place in society. The actual initiation takes place in a series of rituals lasting from November to May. During that time the boys stay in a camp away from their parents and friends, sleeping out in the open and shouting to scare off strangers who happen to come near. There they learn the ancient traditions and practice drumming and Poro songs. They are marked with ritual scars and taken before masked initiates impersonating spirits, the chief of whom is known as the Gbeni. At the end of the training they return to the community as fully fledged adults.

Poro initiates are well aware of the benefits that membership brings, and have some quite cynical stories to account for their beginnings. One tells how, long ago, a chief fell sick with a disease that gave him a harsh nasal whine. Fearing it might be contagious, his people confined him to a hut in the forest.

Some, however, envied his lands and saw a way of turning the situation to their own advantage. First they killed the chief, giving out only that the sickness had finally carried him away. Then they let it be known that his spirit would occasionally come back to the village to visit its family.

To take advantage of the consternation that prospect caused, they devised an instrument out of a hollow stick and a skin membrane that produced a passable imitation of the dead chief's nasal whine. Then they sent a messenger to warn that the spirit was on its way. The villagers took refuge in their huts—but not before they had taken care to leave offerings of rice, goats, and chickens outside to appease the spirit. When they were all safely shut in, the herald circled the village collecting the food, all the while humming into the tube to convince the villagers that it was indeed the chief's spirit that was taking their oblations. And so, the tale-tellers would imply, the Poro's habit of looking after its own got under way.

In Guinea, where the society is also an institution, people tell a story to explain why its members bear ritual scars and expect women to provide them with provisions when they dance. Long ago there was a famine in the land, and the market women were demanding ever higher prices for what little food remained. Driven to desperation, the men decided at a secret meeting to get their hands on the supplies by scaring the women away. So they carved terrifying masks and practiced horrible howls and groans. Then they raided the market, capering and screeching. The women fled in terror, leaving their produce behind in the rush. As for the few men who remained, the dancers seized them and scarified their bodies, saying that this would protect them from the spirits.

In East Africa the nearest equivalent to the secret societies are the hereditary priesthoods, of which that of the Dinka of Sudan is the best known. Even today, Chiefs of the Fishing Spear— so called from the symbols of their office—have great spiritual authority, offering counsel, presiding over ceremonies, and sometimes also acting as law officers.

They too have many legends to describe their beginnings. They tell of a hero called Aiwel, born of a river god and a human mother, who led his people to a promised land then departed for the spirit world—but not before establishing the clans of the Fishing Spear and of the War Spear, whose members would henceforth rule the country.

A helmet-shaped Mende *bundu* mask from the Sande Society, the female equivalent of the well-known male Poro.

The Roles of Men and Women

Along with unfolding the origins of peoples and clans, myths also sought to explain the respective roles of men and women in different societies, and how, for better or worse, they got to be the way they are.

A tone of downbeat realism pervades many African myths about the relationship between individual men and women. "Don't have too high hopes" is the moral they often teach; don't reject a suitor too high-handedly, for you may find the tables turned some day.

One example of this type of story comes in the Ashanti tale of the girl who was captured by "little people"—the African equivalent of fairies. She had just rejected the advances of a hunter, saying he was ugly and covered in ticks. But she had need of a friend when her captors came upon her unawares and started manhandling her.

Hearing her screams, the hunter rushed to her aid and shot her attackers—all except the leader, who promised him whatever he wanted if only he would spare his life and fetch a magic balm to heal the wounds of his injured companions. The hunter obliged, only to find that, once restored to health, the little people had no intention of letting him get away with their possessions. So he and the girl had to race for home, delaying their pursuers by throwing bananas behind them as they went. In this way they reached the safety of the village.

In her gratitude, the girl at once announced that she would gladly wed her rescuer. But now it was his turn to be stubborn. "Tell her I can't marry her," he told her messenger proudly "after all, I still have ticks on my body."

Kikuyu Polygamy

A similarly unromantic note is struck in the Kikuyu's explanation of why their men traditionally had the right to take more than one wife and yet belonged to clans that bore women's names. Things used to be the other way round, the story claimed: in the early times, it was the women who had several husbands. But the men got jealous and plotted revolt.

Among all the Bantu peoples, women adorn themselves with richly beaded necklaces that define their sexuality. The beads here are arranged in a "love-letter" pattern (*ubala abuyisse*), the colors of which encode a secret message. Xhosa, South Africa.

Working in collusion, they saw to it that all the women got pregnant at the same time; then, when the pregnancies lay heavily on them and they were in no position to resist, the men staged a coup and proclaimed themselves in charge.

Their first act was to substitute polygamy for polyandry; in the future it would be the men who had the right to take several spouses. But when they tried to go one step further and substitute male titles for the traditionally female clan names, it was the women's turn to rebel. They let it be known that in future they would kill all male children at birth unless the ancient appellations were retained. In the face of the threat the men backed off, and so realpolitik served to strike a new balance between the sexes.

A Swahili tale about a man who paid an unrealistically high bride-price strikes an equally down-to-earth note. The suitor offered all his assets, in the form of 100 cattle, to secure the hand of a rich man's daughter. The wedding was duly solemnized, but the celebrations were hardly over before the couple realized that they had nothing left to live on. For a while the husband managed to eke out a living for the two of them by milking other people's cows. Then they got word that the bride's father was coming to stay.

This was a disaster, for there was no food left over for a third mouth, let alone for a man used to living well. At this critical moment, the wife ran into a neighborhood seducer who had already made his interest in her very obvious. Now he once more pressed his suit, and in her desperation she promised to give in to his demands, but for a price: a side of beef to feed her father.

Eager to have his way with her, the seducer hurried off to get the meat. He handed it over and started off for home, only to run straight into the husband and father-in-law, who knew nothing of his designs. Convention demanded that the three should stop to exchange pleasantries, and they were still talking when the wife came out to announce that the meal was ready.

Fifteenth-century terracotta figures of a seated man (right) and a kneeling woman, excavated from the ruins of the settlement at Djenne/Mopti between the Niger and Bani rivers.

Seeing them all together, she said, "Come and eat, you three fools." Shocked, the men asked why she addressed them so, and she willingly explained. Her father, she said, was a fool for selling his most treasured possession—his only daughter—for 100 cattle when he already had 6,000. The husband was worse for giving all he had and leaving nothing for them to live on. And the suitor was the biggest fool of all for thinking he could buy for a single side of beef what had already been sold for 100 cattle.

On hearing his designs exposed, the lecher ran off and never troubled the couple again. The father too was chastened and sent back the bride-price, giving the two all they needed to live comfortably together. So the woman's quick tongue saved the marriage.

71

Learning Lessons from the Animals

Animal fables are among the most popular of all African stories. The tales may be comic or solemn, but the picture of life that they paint is usually remarkably unsentimental.

Those stories involving the tortoise and the hare are well known (see pages 108–109), but there are many other African fables: some set out to explain how animals got their characteristics, while others are morality tales aimed at humankind.

The Leopard's Spots

Typical of the first kind are the stories describing how the leopard obtained its spots. According to an amusing version from Sierra Leone, it happened when, at his wife's insistence, Leopard foolishly invited his friend Fire to their house. He no longer had a home left afterward, but the scorch marks on his skin have remained to this day.

The Tumbuka of Malawi say that the spots were painted on by Tortoise, who owed Leopard a favor for rescuing him from a tree. In similar vein, Tortoise went on to beautify Zebra by painting on his stripes; but when Hyena, who had originally put him up the tree as a joke, came for the same treatment, he was given the ugly pelt he has retained ever since.

The First Elephant

A curious Kamba tale from Kenya explains the origin of elephants. A poor man who wanted to become rich was sent for advice to a famously wealthy benefactor named Ivonya-Ngia. This man thought for a while, and then gave him an ointment, telling him to smear it on his wife's canine teeth. They would grow to an unusual size; then he had merely to extract and sell them.

The poor man did as he was told, and was delighted when, in a few weeks' time, her canines turned into tusks of ivory. He pulled them out and got a good price for them, then repeated the process. Soon he was as rich as he could have wished.

His success aroused the envy of his neighbor, who asked how he too could make money. The first man directed him to Ivonya-Ngia, who gave him the same ointment but neglected to mention anything about tooth-pulling. As a result, the man let his

While renowned and respected for its power and strength, the leopard was also considered by many ordinary people to be a bully, lacking wisdom and intelligence. Snarling leopard plaque that formerly decorated the palace of the *obas* of Benin.

The Crest and the Hide

A Lega story from Congo points an uncompromising moral about the limits of friendship.

A lizard and a guinea-fowl lived in a village where the people took it in turns to be chief. When the lizard's time came, it did everything possible to ensure that its investiture was suitably splendid. It got a ceremonial drum, a magnificent outfit, a hide to sit on, and plenty of beer to refresh the onlookers.

All that remained was a suitable headdress. Wanting a splendid plume to top it, it sent word to its friend the guinea-fowl. The bird presented it with feathers of every shape and size, but none would do, for the lizard had already decided that it would only be satisfied with the guinea-fowl's own splendid crest. Eventually the bird unwillingly had it cut off—leaving guinea-fowl looking shorn ever since.

In time the lizard's term ended and the guinea-fowl's own turn arrived. It too sought to do everything grandly, gathering the necessary drum, drink, and finery to wear. But again something was missing—this time a hide. So the bird demanded one from the lizard—and, on a quid pro quo basis, insisted that none would do but the lizard's own. Public opinion sided with the fowl over the request, so the lizard eventually had to agree to be skinned, with fatal results. A Lega proverb spells out the moral: Don't ask a friend for more than he can give.

wife's tusks grow so large that her entire face and body were transformed and she became an elephant. Eventually she left their hut and went to live in the forest. From her the elephant race descended—and they are still as clever as people.

Two Honey-loving Birds

Some stories straddle the gap between the myth of origin and the moral fable. One example is a Baila tale that explains the different destiny of two bird species: the honey-guide, which is esteemed by humans for showing them where to find honey, and the wheat-ear, which is trapped with birdlime. In early times they lived together, and one day went in search of honey. They found a honeycomb and noted the spot, planning to return the next morning. But in the meantime the wheat-ear slipped out and ate all the honey itself.

When the two returned to the spot the next day, only a few bits of the comb remained. Angrily the honey-guide accused the wheat-ear of having eaten it, but the other bird protested its innocence. When they subsequently found another honeycomb, the wheat-ear, to bolster its story, insisted that they should put birdlime around it to see who the thief really was. The honey-guide agreed, and the two went off to get some from the human beings who made it. Returning home with their purchase, they agreed to lay it the following morning. Only this time the honey-guide stole off to set the lime early. When the wheat-ear then tried to repeat its trick, it got stuck and died.

The next day the honey-guide found the corpse and drew the moral. The wheat-ear would thieve no more; and people would in the future cherish honey-guides as helpers, while for wheat-ears they would have only contempt—and birdlime.

Lessons for Humankind

Some Ethiopian fables are similarly bleak in their worldview, but express it wryly. One tells how a leopard cub strayed from home and was killed when an elephant accidentally stepped on it. As soon as news of the tragedy reached the father, he swore revenge. But when he heard that the guilty party was a bull elephant, he momentarily hung back; an image of its huge bulk crossed his mind.

Then, he made his feelings known decisively. "No," he roared. "You're wrong. It was a goat that did this terrible deed!" And he at once rushed off and killed a large number of goats grazing peacefully in the neighboring hills. The point, needless to say, applies also to the human world: when a man is wronged by a person stronger than himself, he will often seek revenge on someone weaker.

A similar tale recounts what happened when a lion, a leopard, a hyena, and a donkey came together to bemoan their condition in the midst of a terrible drought. Food was getting scarce, and between them they tried to work out why. Eventually they decided that it must be divine judgement on their sins, and reckoned it would be best for them all to confess their wrong-doing.

The lion admitted to the heinous offense of killing and eating a young bull near a village, but the other animals, fearing his strength, hastened to assure him that that was no sin. The leopard then said that it had savaged a goat it found wandering away from its herd; once more the consensus was

This ceremonial sword and sheath, known as the udamalore, *belonged to the ruler of the Owo-Yoruba peoples. It had military and magical prowess because of its powerful animal motifs.*

that there was nothing to repent. The hyena had stolen into a village to seize a chicken; but again the animals saw no harm.

Then it was the donkey's turn. The worst fault it could come up with was nibbling a few blades of grass while its owner wasn't looking. But none of the other beasts feared the donkey, so despite the triviality of the offense they all joined in saying, "That is a terrible sin. You have caused all our suffering." And so they killed and ate the inoffensive beast, illustrating the bitter moral that it is usually the powerless who end up getting the blame.

By no means are all African animal tales so pessimistic. A narrative from the Ngbandi people of the Congo region has an upbeat message about the strength that can come from cooperation and community. It describes how an elephant went on a hunting trip with a tiny dudu bird. At the end of the day they wanted to let their respective wives know they were coming home so that each could start getting a meal ready. The elephant trumpeted with all its might, and a great wave of sound swept through the glade. But the bird could only feebly cheep its distinctive *dudu, dudu.*

A second bird nearer home heard the notes, however, and took up the cry. That was picked up by a third, and so on; thus the call passed swiftly through the forest. When the two got back to the bird's house, dinner was ready and waiting.

The bird invited his friend to join him, but the elephant declined, saying that he was expecting a large meal in his own home nearby. Only when he got there, he found nothing at all. Because of the distance, his wife had not heard the trumpeting.

There are many stories in which the weak defeat the strong. One from Malawi's Namwanga people uses the familiar animal-helper theme. It tells how a hunter lifted a shrew across a ditch, for which the profusely grateful animal promised to assist him in return if it ever got the chance. The man and his dogs then killed some guinea-fowl.

Late in the day it rained and the hunter took shelter in a hut. The tiny shrew, which had followed him, hid in the thatch. Before long a lion came along. Scenting the man, it roared out: "Give the guinea-fowl to the dogs to eat—then you eat the dogs and I'll eat you!" The man quaked, thinking his final hour had come. But the shrew had other ideas. In a small but determined voice, it squeaked out: "That's right. Give the guinea-fowl to the dogs to eat, then you eat the dogs, the lion will eat you—and I'll eat the lion!" And with that the lion turned tail and fled.

DEATH'S RICH RITUAL

Humankind's hold on life was precarious throughout Africa, with famine, virulent diseases, and dangerous animals a constant danger. Mortality itself was believed to stem from some mistake or other on the part of the first people rather than having been part of the original, divinely ordained creation. The demise of infants or senior citizens was understood, but anything more untimely that occured during a person's prime was invariably considered to be the work of evil forces. Death, however, was not usually accepted as the end of existence, merely the loss of corporeal form: the invisible spirit lived on ready to manifest itself in dreams or another body, either human or animal. Funerary practices differed, although most people believed the spirit remained near the place of death or burial—even living on, perhaps, within a predatory animal that may have caused the person's demise.

Below: Malagasy funerary practices are complex. In the south, among the Mahafaly, decorated posts are used to adorn the graves. These elaborate *aloalo* show human figures with full and half-moon motifs surmounted by a bird or zebu. Related *ajiba* cenotaphs show scenes from the deceased's life.

Above: A copper-covered *mbulu ngulu* reliquary piece from the Kota people of Congo and Gabon. The *ngulu* was placed to watch over the basket containing the bones of an ancestor.

Right: A wooden memorial screen or *nduen fobara* ("forehead of the dead"), from a West African household ancestral shrine. Spirits of dead family members were believed to enter the figures represented and could thus receive the sacrifices and prayers of descendants. The headdresses revealed details about the deceased's social status. Kalabari, Niger Delta region, late 19th century.

HEROES AND TRICKSTERS

Unruly and mischievous Legba, the Fon's divine trickster, once deceived and humiliated the great creator Mawu-Lisa. Legba was cross that people on Earth blamed him for evil while praising Mawu-Lisa for all that was good—and, worse still, Mawu-Lisa approved of this state of affairs. But Legba plotted sweet revenge. First he spread the word that thieves were planning to steal the yams from Mawu-Lisa's garden; as he expected, Mawu-Lisa announced that whoever was caught with them would face execution. By night Legba went into the garden wearing Mawu-Lisa's sandals and left many footprints as he took the tubers. At the morning inquest it appeared as if Mawu-Lisa had stolen her own yams and the high goddess-god was embarrassed in front of her people.

Mischief pure and simple looms large in Africa's trickster stories. The trickster delights in its own cunning, in provoking conflict and undermining order. Often an insect or an animal, they include the ever-resourceful spider Ananse and the wild, springing hare. Through slavery, both traveled to the Americas and Caribbean, with the hare acquiring fame as Brer Rabbit. Among the Fon and Yoruba, on the other hand, the trickster is one of the gods.

Sometimes their mischief brings good things—such as magic and useful charms—into the world. Other exploits explain the first appearance of a bad thing—Ananse's foolery leads to the spread of disease among the tribes on Earth. But their antics always exist for their own sake or to prove the trickster's cool cunning and resourcefulness. They never have a higher purpose.

The tricksters therefore stand in contrast to the culture heroes who feature in many myths of tribal origin. The culture hero is an ancestor who taught the people the skills necessary for survival in their particular conditions. In Congo, the Mongo-Nkundo lived by hunting, taught to them by their culture hero. The principal culture hero of the agricultural Dogon of Mali was a blacksmith who brought to Earth from Heaven the knowledge of ironmaking that enabled them to forge tools with which to tame the hardy landscape. By contrast with the slippery trickster, the culture hero is more straightforwardly benign: he may have flaws, but his achievement is that his descendants establish themselves in the landscape and survive to celebrate his name.

Above: Elephant masks were used in many parts of Africa, often to represent the connections between rulers and the forces of nature. *Ogbodo enyi*, "village friend" mask, Igbo, Nigeria.

Opposite: The mischief-making monkey was said to have annoyed the leopard so much it was beaten and thereafter took to sleeping in trees in order to avoid the big cat. Carved monkey figure representing an initiation ceremony drummer, Nkanu people, Kwango, Congo.

The Epic Songs of the Bards

The inhabitants of the Sahel grasslands of western Africa share a tradition of ancient epic poetry. The poems date from the fourth to twelfth centuries, but look back to an older time perhaps 1,000 years before, and are sung by bards or griots closely associated with the noble clans of their peoples.

The influential Bamana-Malinke groups tell a poignant myth of how the first bard was inspired to celebrate the achievements of his tribesmen in the enduring form of song. Long, long ago two brothers, driven by hunger, trailed deep into the bush in search of game. But the herds were elusive and although the men were skilled hunters they could not pick up the track of any animals. The sun beat down on them and on the bush, which had been stripped bare of fruits and edible plants by the intense heat.

After spending three days searching in vain for food, they realized that they had lost their bearings and could not find their way back to their village. The older brother was the weaker of the two and now he slumped down on a hard rock, wincing as he looked up into the bright light. In a frail voice he informed his brother that he was too exhausted to go a step farther. Hunger had drained him of strength and even the will to live. He was ready for bony Death to take him.

The younger brother's heart ached to see his closest ally in such distress. His legs shook, but he thrust his chest forward and declared that he would not abandon him. Rest there on the rock, he told his brother; meanwhile, he proposed, he himself would go ahead and search for food.

The younger left the older and went on into the murderous heat. The day was perfectly still and nothing stirred for countless miles around. There was no way of finding food, but he could not allow his own brother to die of starvation. So he took his carving knife, pulled his loincloth from his thigh, and sliced some flesh from his upper leg. Then he carefully concealed the wound beneath his loincloth and went back to where his brother lay sprawled. He pretended to be the bearer of good news, claiming that he had lain in wait and pounced on a small bush animal. He showed his brother the red, dripping meat that would save him from death.

The younger brother made a fire, cooked the meat, and fed his ailing sibling who ate greedily. Afterward the older one regained his strength and the brothers walked on in the dust. When, before long, they saw smoke rising, they knew there must be a settlement this side of the horizon. Slowly they proceeded, hope returning, but the older brother stopped when he saw blood staining the other's loincloth. He asked what was the matter but his brother turned away, avoiding the subject.

The older brother was insistent and caught hold of his sibling. He pulled at the cloth until he could see the wound—and then it became clear to him what his brother had done. He clasped him in his arms and spoke momentous words. The gift of his brother's flesh had saved him from extinction, so from that day, he said, he would become a bard to sing of his younger brother's deeds and make his name live forever. He pledged that his descendants would serve his younger brother's posterity down the generations as bards. Because of the younger brother's deed of fraternal love, his family's name would live forever and his reputation would be immortal.

In the central act of the younger brother caring for the older one, the story alludes to issues of legitimacy and precedence, suggesting younger brothers can take power in place of their elders.

Traditional, cone-shaped dwellings in a village along the Niger River in the Sahel provide a sense of the region's space and climate. Many groups spanning the area, such as the Soninke, Fulani, Wolof, Mandinka, Malinke, Bamana, and Songhay, share the epic poetic tradition.

The Talking Drum

Drums, once found in every African village, were used both for communication and for dances of celebration.

Yoruba drum with a motif alluding to female fertility, 19th century.

In traditional African society the king or chief had a special drum on which his commands and communications could be issued by his appointed drummer. Aside from the king and the drummer, nobody else could touch it. Possession of the drum was an important mark of prestige: in Burundi when a new king came to power he showed his authority by placing his feet on the king's drum. In some traditions the royal drums were locked away after a king's death and a new set made for his successor.

The language of the drum was a sensitive one and long messages or even poems could be beaten out. Traditionally among the Akan peoples of Ghana ceremonial occasions were marked by the performance of eulogies, proverbs, and other poems on the drum. In almost all traditions drummers at a feast would lead dances both ceremonial and social.

Drummers who sent messages out across the dense forest or open country—a form of public announcement—used a code that was understood only by their kinsmen in other settlements. Those who lived close to borders with other tribal groups would have had to learn more than one drum code so that they could translate from one to another. Drum hide might be of elephant or antelope skin; split drums gave different tones, a higher and lower, from their two halves.

People believed that each drum had a spirit. A drum-maker would perform special ceremonies when he went to the forest to select the wood for the casing. He prayed that the spirit of the tree would not flee the wood when it was cut and would remain to give life and a voice to the instrument. Drums could not be passed among many owners or performers, for the spirit might take offense.

The Story of Prince Gassire's Lute

The account of how a princely warrior was distracted from battle by the lure of song may be a surviving fragment of one of the Soninke epics. In ancient times Prince Gassire (*gesere* is a Soninke word for bard or griot) of the Fasa, an aristocratic people from the coast, fought daily in the army of his father King Nganamba against the Burdama. He was the greatest warrior on either side, and was loudly celebrated for his deeds on the battlefield—but he was not satisfied, for his father was old and he longed to be king himself. Gassire had already waited a long time, for he had eight sons grown to adulthood.

Beneath the sun Gassire lost himself in the frenzy of war, but in the courts of night he knew no peace, for the desire to be king ate at his heart like a jackal chewing on a fallen antelope. One night he consulted a seer, who pronounced his destiny: Gassire would never be king, for he would abandon his sword for the lute of a bard; his father would die, but others would take the kingship and their great city would fall. Gassire leaped up in anger, refusing to believe the unwelcome prediction. But the wise old man insisted it would come true, for it was destined so: Gassire would go to the fields and understand the song of the partridges; forever after he would desire the path of the bard and have the greatest respect for the enduring power of song.

Destiny shaped Gassire's life as the old man had foreseen. The following day the hero sent his fellow soldiers back to the city and alone sought conflict with the Burdama. Against all-comers he triumphed with spear and sword. His reputation as a warrior could reach no higher. But that very night he was drawn to wander in the fields and heard and understood the song of the partridge. The bird sang of how warriors and even kings died and their bodies rotted in the ground, but the epic song of the bards endured for ever. A city might fall and rise, a tribe could abandon one site and build a great new city somewhere else, but the song would never change and never die.

Gassire ordered a craftsman to make him a lute. The man warned that it would not issue music, but Gassire dismissed what he said. Yet, sure enough, when the lute was made it would not sound. He returned it to the craftsman, who said that the spirit in the wood would not consent to sing until Gassire had taken the lute into battle over his shoulder and allowed it to absorb the smell of conflict and the blood of heroes.

The prince carried the lute with his shield, spears, and sword onto the battlefield, where he fought wildly. One after another, his seven oldest sons died—and as he carried them back to the city their blood dripped onto the lute. Finally the people of the city wanted no more: they told Gassire that he fought without reason, in a mere frenzy, and they were not willing to support him any longer. Gassire took his wives and friends, his only surviving son and his lute and rode far into the grim Sahara Desert. One night as the others slept beneath the endless stars he heard the lute sing and he proclaimed the first of many epics of the men of Fasa. That very night far away King Nganamba died and the great city fell to its enemies, as foretold.

Accoutrements of war, such as a sword and arrows or spears, accompany ancestor figures on this West African granary shutter. Crops and territory required constant protection from enemies, and the epic struggles that ensued were celebrated in both Gassire's songs and those of other Sahel peoples.

Wonderful Children

Many African peoples recount the history of a child born fully equipped to survive, with precocious wits, the strength of an adult, and the ability to talk at birth. The child's name differs, but his wonderful attributes and achievements add color to many traditions.

The wonderful child usually has to start life by out-witting his own mother, for the tales commonly begin with the mother promising her unborn baby to a monster, demon, or flesh-crazed beast: after the birth the child escapes despite his mother's best efforts to honor her promise. Usually she abandons her maternal instincts because her own life is in danger, but sometimes she does it in order to satisfy a craving that is tormenting her heart.

After the birth the wondrous child tells his mother to hold him over the flames of a fire—a tradition among some Bantu peoples. In some versions this accounts for the name given to the child. The Bantu Hehe call him Galinkalanganye ("The One Held Over the Fire"); among the Yao he is known as Kalikalanje, a name derived from the Hehe name. Congo's Nyanga call him Kachirambe.

Kachirambe's Birth

Quick-witted Kachirambe was born in the following, unusual way. A girl found an egg belonging to a hyena in the bush, put it in her basket, and took it home. (The tale does not account for the fact of a hyena having an egg, but in African folklore the hyena was commonly associated with the strange

and unexplained—the strong-jawed beast with its ugly "laugh" could imitate a human voice, but was also renowned for its stupidity.) The girl's mother threw it on the fire. The hyena found its way to the house and confronted the mother, who said that the egg had burned up, but in its place promised to hand over the next child she had.

Every day the hyena visited to ask when the child would be delivered. Finally it barked a warning that if the baby was not forthcoming it would feast on the mother's flesh instead. Within a few days the anxious mother noticed a swelling on her shin; it grew more and more bulbous until it burst. Then in a blaze of light emerged a remarkable boy child. Straight away he could walk and talk, and he emerged in her dusty hut armed with bow and arrow and with hunting dogs clamoring at his heels. In a deep voice, he announced that he was Kachirambe, the shin-bone's child. The strange birth is matched in other traditions: the great Lianja of the Mongo-Nkundo was born in the same way (see page 91).

Kachirambe's mother knew she could not evade the hyena and when the beast approached, she announced that she had given birth to a child, but warned that the boy was too clever to be caught. Sure enough, although she conspired with the hyena to trap her own son, Kachirambe was always too cunning and quickly managed to outwit and kill the beast. When confronted, his mother begged forgiveness and her son graciously laid the past aside.

Hyena-like hunting dogs, associated with Kachirambe, are believed to mediate between both humans and animals and the dead and the living, helping to regulate the world. Double-headed *nkondi* power figure, Congo.

The Little Boy and the Monster

The Basuto, another Bantu people, tell of a marvelous, warlike child born to his mother in a time of direst need, when the fearsome beast Khodumodumo was terrorizing the people.

Hideous Khodumodumo arose from the country beyond the mountains to prey on the Basuto. Squeezing through a mountain pass, it came into a wide valley where many villages nestled. There it went on a rampage of killing, consuming every living thing that it encountered, whether beast, bird, or human.

Finally only one woman was left. She was heavily pregnant and her survival instinct was strong. She smeared her body with white ashes and hid herself

by squatting in an animal pen. The beast passed by but, swollen with the bodies of villagers, it stuck fast in the mountain pass.

That very afternoon the woman gave birth to a boy. She laid him gently on the ground and turned away; when she looked back, it was to find a fully grown man grasping spears in his hands and wearing around his neck a string of bones used for divination. She demanded to know the baby's whereabouts, but the man insisted that he was her child, miraculously grown. His name was Moshanyana ("Little Boy").

He asked where the villagers were and she explained about the beast's depradations. Moshanyana proudly rose and, seeing Khodumodumo unable to squeeze through the pass, went to confront it. The monster tried to swallow Moshanyana but the warrior skipped away; the beast could hardly move and it was swift work for the warrior to kill it with sword and spear. As he cut into the swollen belly of the monster, he heard a man's voice cry out, and another—then a cock crowed and a cow lowed deep. Feverishly he sliced and was able to free all the animals, men and women of the villages. That night the valley resounded with celebrations.

Lonkundo the Hunter

The Mongo-Nkundo, a hunting people from the densely forested central part of the Congo basin, preserved mythical histories of a tribal founder and culture hero named Lonkundo. The first hunter, he taught his people the skills of trapping and tracking the forest beasts.

Lonkundo learned how to hunt from his father's spirit. It came in a dream and told him to go to the local well in the light of dawn and look for the track of a wild animal. Once he had found it, he should make a trap from raffia fibers and twigs and set it for the beast. With his father's guidance, Lonkundo made and set the first trap in the Congo. Over the following weeks he traveled far and wide, setting his traps and killing many beasts. Lonkundo became wealthy and all the villagers regarded him with respect. But he was troubled by powerful dreams, and one night as he slept he imagined he had caught the sun itself in his trap. Then a few days later he saw a brilliant light through the trees. He approached silently with the lithe step of a hunter and saw that one of his traps had indeed caught a remarkable prey—a woman of radiant beauty.

Hunters need reliable tools. This Kota throwing knife evokes a bird's head, in reference perhaps to the power of flight.

She told him that she was a king's daughter who had refused many suitors but had then been lured into the forest by a handsome traveler. Deep in the shadowy wastes, among crowding trees, he had vanished and she had wandered despairingly until she fell into the trap. Her name was Ilankaka, she said, and her father would pay a handsome reward to the man who brought her back. But Lonkundo told her that he wanted no reward other than to have her as his wife. Ilankaka

agreed to this at once and went with him, but she warned her captor that he should never boast of having caught her in his trap—or trouble would befall them.

Back in his village Ilankaka settled into Lonkundo's home alongside his first wife, Nsombe, and their son Yonjwa. With Ilankaka's encouragement, he took other wives from surrounding settlements to reflect his status. Among the Mongo-Nkundo and many other African peoples it was customary for an important man to have several wives; the first or most senior of the women gained status from having juniors to wait on them and so encouraged their husband to marry often.

But the people of Lonkundo's own village grew jealous of his success and when he heard them speaking coldly of him, the great hunter resolved to leave. The very next morning, in the gentle starlight before dawn, he and his large family set off into the unknown.

They traveled deep into the overgrown forest. On the first night, as the women rested, Lonkundo set off to hunt. He encountered a tall, mysterious man who was calling "Lonkundo! Lonkundo! Lonkundo!" The hunter wounded and bound the tall stranger, then took him back to the camp, where Ilankaka identified the man as the handsome traveler who had abandoned her deep in the forest long before. Lonkundo gave him to Ilankaka to be her manservant.

The next morning they traveled on, then halted in a place where Ilankaka heard screeching parrots—for she identified this as a good omen. Here, she declared, they should build their new settlement. Now a sacrifice was needed to appease the local spirits; Lonkundo and Ilankaka agreed that her new manservant should be slaughtered. He went to his death without complaint and then Lonkundo set the slaves to work cutting down the towering trees from which they would build the huts of their new village.

Lonkundo quarreled with his first wife, Nsombe, after she complained that she was not satisfied with her hut. She left the settlement to live alone with Yonjwa, her son by Lonkundo. Ilankaka was pleased, for she saw the quarrel as a sign that her husband loved her best of all. In her delight she showed him a magic nut her father had given her with instructions to plant it on the day she was sure of her husband's love. She set the kernel in the ground and a magnificent palm grew beside their hut. The fruits they picked from it were ravishing to the taste.

But when Lonkundo asked for more nuts to share with his other wives and children, Ilankaka refused him, saying that the results of her father's magic were for the two of them alone. He lost his temper and loudly reminded her that he had once had her at his mercy when she cowered in his trap. In the terrible silence that followed, he saw that he had broken the only unbreakable rule of their life together. Ilankaka never spoke to him again. She took her things and disappeared.

Some time later Lonkundo sought out Nsombe in the heart of the forest and asked her forgiveness. On that day Nsombe and Yonjwa returned to the main settlement. Lonkundo saw that Yonjwa had grown into a virile young man and told him that the time had come for him too to seek a wife.

The radiantly beautiful Ilankaka was one of Lonkundo's more unusual prey. This southern Congo *chokwe* mask epitomizes female beauty. The scars signify ethnic membership.

Son of Death

When Lonkundo's son Yonjwa started a family of his own, his first-born was a mysterious being named Itonde, an incarnation of dread Death itself. Itonde's son Lianja was the hero of a new phase of the myth cycle.

There are many variations of the cycle of Lonkundo and Lianja, and the feats of Itonde belong to one of these. It recounts how long ago, before the tribes had found their settlements, Yonjwa and his wife Eyonga lived deep in the forest, at a place named Ngimokili ("The World's Center"). They kept with them a magic pouch that Eyonga had brought from her father's village; it would save her descendants many times.

Eyonga became pregnant and would eat only rat's flesh. Her unborn child, Itonde, emerged by night from his mother's belly without her knowing; daylight would send him scurrying back. But one morning he banished the sun by creating darkness. Eyonga felt her stomach flatten and assumed sadly that she had miscarried, but then she and Yonjwa encountered their wild child in the pantry as he was stealing their supplies of smoked rat. He attacked them with burning spittle and they ran from their house, never to return.

Itonde, associated with darkness and the rats found by decaying bodies, was Death itself. He lived alone, killing passing animals by throwing palm nuts at them. Then one day, as he was about to kill a hummingbird, the bird spoke, begging for mercy. When Itonde explained that he had been abandoned in the forest, the hummingbird fetched a magical caterpillar-bird from a nearby tree. It gave Itonde a bell, which it said contained all life and was the world itself; if he were ever in any danger, he need only ring it to be saved.

Itonde then decided to leave the forest. He came to Yonjwa's village and laid claim to the great man as his father. Yonjwa and the villagers made the boy drink poison to prove that he was telling the truth, and he survived the ordeal. Then Yonjwa treated his long-lost son lavishly.

In one version Itonde traveled to find a wife and came back with Mbombe. While they were returning to the village, Itonde and Mbombe quarreled repeatedly and both several times ran off into the forest. On one occasion, Itonde was startled by creatures and ran away from them—but then, looking more closely, he saw what they were and gave them the names used ever since by the sons and daughters of the tribe.

Itonde and the Serpent

Itonde's sister-in-law fell pregnant and craved snake's flesh. With his brother Lofale, Itonde set off into the dense forest to look for some. They found a great serpent entwined about a tree. Itonde tried to lure it down with song, but it would not come. With night falling, Itonde feared what the serpent might do under cover of darkness and set a trap to prevent the sun dropping below the horizon. He was burned to death, but the hand that held his magic bell survived and brought him back to life by ringing it.

Finally he persuaded the snake to descend and he brought the heavy serpent to the village. As he lowered it to the ground, in a single movement the snake whipped its body around the settlement and swallowed everyone. Furious, Itonde killed it, but just before it died the snake warned him to eat it whole—or rue the consequences. He managed to consume the vast body but could not finish the head. In the night the snake came back to life and tried to crush him, but he woke in time and banished it with the bell. In the morning, the snake's spirit visited him and said that it would now help him. It showed Itonde a beautiful new village, where he settled with Mbombe.

How the Sun Rises and Falls

Lianja sent the bright-eyed sparrowhawk to the great god Yemekonji high in Heaven to find the sun's divinely ordained position. Luckily, the brave bird was preceded by the humble fly.

The fly chose to accompany the sparrowhawk on its mission. It proposed that it would go on ahead and eavesdrop in Heaven in case Yemekonji's councilors were preparing a surprise.

When the fly arrived, it heard of a plan to hide the sun in one of three parcels. Two colorful ones would be filled with leaves and earth respectively; the third, in plain wrapping, would contain the sun. Thus the fly forewarned the bird.

When the sparrowhawk approached Yemekonji, the great god complained that two previous deputations had come from Earth seeking the sun: the first man had chosen the evening star, while the second had taken the moon. Yemekonji asked the sparrowhawk whether he was hiding a spy and the bird, praising his host's wisdom, insisted it came alone; Yemekonji in any case knew about the fly.

Then the sparrowhawk was offered the choice of the three parcels and, remembering the fly's advice, chose the plainly wrapped one that contained the sun. Yemekonji was not upset and instructed the bird how to ease the sun into its orbit in the realm of the windkissed clouds. He went on to explain that from that time the sun would disappear and reappear in a regular pattern.

Down from Heaven hurtled the bird, its beak gripping the parcel; when it came among the clouds it swiftly opened the wrapping, releasing the bright ball—which rolled away across the long spaces of the air.

Upon reaching Earth, the bird explained that Yemekonji had plotted the sun's movements so it would set after twelve hours, then twelve hours later rise once more. Forever after it has followed this divine cycle.

Mbombe's Craving

In time Mbombe became pregnant, and when she tasted an unfamiliar nut dropped by a passing bird she developed a craving for more. She pestered Itonde to fetch some, but he did not know where they were to be found. It was the hornbill who showed him that the nuts grew on the sausau tree, but the bird also warned Itonde that a man named Fetefete stood guard over them day and night. Sure enough, when Itonde arrived the man tried to stop him, but he nonetheless managed to return with a great haul of nuts.

Itonde's actions gave the forest birds their bright plumage. West African Baga people's headdress, 19th century.

Mbombe had soon eaten them all and begged for more. Two more times Itonde went to the sausau tree and succeeded in taking the fruits. Fetefete, the local villagers, and their chief, named Sau Sau, tried to stop him by sending birds to attack the thief high in the tree. But he threw nuts at them to drive them off—and the missiles changed the birds' coloring where they hit their feathers. In this way, all the multi-colored birds of the tropical forest were given their appearances. On the second occasion the birds almost made him tumble from the tree, but he rang his magic bell, summoning thunder and lightning to drive his attackers away.

Again Mbombe begged Itonde to fetch her nuts. Before he left, he warned the villagers that if they saw a wound rope uncurl and an elephant walk through the village, it would mean that he had met his end. At the sausau tree, many animals and birds had gathered to defend the nuts. A blue pheasant attacked Itonde, and he was unable to drive it off. He rang his bell but it shattered and he knew that his last hour had come. Falling, he landed in a net laid by the steadfast turtle. Far away in his own village, an elephant emerged from the forest and a rope uncurled. The villagers cried with astonishment that mighty Itonde could have been bested. But Mbombe could not mourn, for her labor had begun.

Itonde's body rotted away very rapidly. The birds pecked at it, and from it worms and maggots slithered out. Brown water also oozed from the places where the birds had bitten, and as the liquid ran away into the ground it formed marshland and marsh rivers.

Lianja Is Born

Meanwhile Mbombe's body was arched in labor, racked with pain. Flies, wasps, ants, bees, and other insects crawled from her belly—the first insects the world had known. From her abundant womb were born Balumbe, Bafoto, Bielangi, Mbole, Nkundo, and Elinga, the six ancestors of the Mongo-speaking tribes of Central Africa.

Itonde's corpse decayed and oozed away, becoming the marshy waters of the Congo River—the longest in Africa after the Nile.

Then Mbombe delivered a radiant daughter named Nsongo. The women relaxed, believing the marathon labor to be over. But then a deep voice rang out from Mbombe's womb, and asked how it could get out. Mbombe told the child within her to exit the same way as its predecessors, but it countered proudly that it was a king's son and could not follow another's path. It ordered her to have some of its father's ceremonial white clay applied to her shin. Once the clay was in place the shin began to swell and open. Mbombe howled in agony. From her leg emerged a man armed with a bow and knife, holding the chiefly staff, wearing the king's necklace and carrying a bell and horn.

In the first hour of Lianja's life on Earth his blood pulsed with the desire to avenge his father's death. His mother was reluctant to reveal how Itonde had died, for she did not want to lose her newborn to Sau Sau. But Lianja pestered her until she revealed the truth.

Lianja pressed the men of the village into an army. Before he left, Mbombe passed on to him the magic pouch of Eyonga. The men marched off and eventually they came to the place where the sausau tree grew. A message went to Sau Sau that Itonde's son had come to seek revenge, and he marched at once to the clearing. Lianja sent in detachments of insects, but they were repulsed. Then the two armies fought, spilling a river of blood. At last only the two leaders remained. Face-to-face they stood and for a moment the air was still. Then Lianja encouraged Sau Sau to attack with his spears. The first drove deep into Lianja's heart; he fell but then clapped his hands and the spear withdrew, leaving him unharmed. Sau Sau used all his weapons but none did any harm. Then Lianja sliced off Sau Sau's head.

He stood, chest heaving, looking about at the bloody carnage in the forest. The very trees seemed to turn away. Lianja took the magic pouch and slowly toured the battlefield, gently lifting the head of each of his dead warriors and rubbing their nostrils with a little of the powder. Every last one sneezed and awoke to life.

Then magnanimous Lianja brought Sau Sau and his warriors back to life too. They agreed to submit to him and became his willing followers. He was a powerful king with many subject peoples. In time he married and had many fine children; the favorite was his daughter Yendembe, whom he spoiled with an overindulgent love.

The Death of Lianja

But even great Lianja's glorious reign had to end. The king was killed over a few fish. He came upon a stream in his territory where a fisherman named Ngimokeli had rigged up a clever dam that backed up the fish into nets. Lianja took some, for he saw that the nets would soon burst—and in any case he considered it his right to do so. But when Ngimokeli leaped up and insulted Mbombe, the two men fought and both were killed.

In another version, Lianja did not die but led the tribes on a forest procession; different peoples stopped in various places and founded their ancestral homelands. He settled on the banks of the Congo with his sister and they live there still.

91

The Blacksmith Culture Heroes

Among the ancestors the first to learn the secrets of ironmaking held an important place, for this craft made possible the hard-edged tools with which people tamed the landscape as well as the sharp weapons with which they went to war. In most traditions the first blacksmith was at least partly divine, bringing knowledge of iron down from Heaven.

The Dogon held that a primeval ancestor brought knowledge of the forge, of iron tools, and of husbandry from Heaven to Earth. At the same time he carried fire down from the heavenly smithy worked by the divine Nummo twins (see page 43). He was said to be one of eight ancestors; in some accounts all eight were Nummos, and either took an androgynous form or were male-female twins. From Heaven the first blacksmith rode down the rainbow in a ship in the shape of a granary. With him, he brought a hammer and anvil, and the hammer contained all the seeds he was to teach men and women how to plant with. The blacksmith's original shape resembled that of the Nummos, with sleek arms and legs like fronds of vegetation. But when his ship landed with a crash, both his arms and legs were bent. The impact gave him elbows and knees, but this transformation was right and proper, for with an elbow he could exert greater power to pound on the anvil or dig at the hard ground. He taught the first people, his descendants, how to make tools as well as how to clear and plant fields of crops.

Among the Dogon the blacksmith was greatly respected and even had a religious function. In an

Edan ogboni **paired brass insignia (male and female), whose power derives in part from an iron stake set in the base. Yoruba, 19th century.**

important ceremony that marked the first days of the season for sowing crops, the blacksmith beat the ground with his anvil while a goat was sacrificed. According to Ogotemmeli, a blind Dogon initiate who revealed some of his people's religious mythology in the mid-twentieth century, the blacksmith's action enabled a divine force to pass from the Earth into the liver of the goat and thence into the man who ate the liver—once it was cooked—as part of the ritual.

Ogun, the Yoruba Iron God

Many Yoruba myths detail the exploits of the divine *orishas* and the first humans at the dawn of history. The roles played by particular *orishas* differ according to local traditions, for the mythology is closely allied to founding stories told of particular kingdoms. But all agree that it was the divine blacksmith Ogun who taught both gods and men how to make iron tools, how to hunt, and how to clear the forest to create crop-bearing fields.

It happened at a time when *orishas* and humans needed to expand their domain, for they were pressed up hard against the forest edge.

A number of *orishas* tried to clear space for fields, but they only had tools of soft metal or even wood and they could not hack down the crowding trees. Even Eshu, mischievous trickster and master of languages, could not prevail against the trees.

Then Ogun set to with his iron knife, the only one on Earth. With this marvelous weapon he took on the forest and cleared a great expanse of fields. The other *orishas* begged for knowledge of the tool that did not twist or bend. But Ogun declared that the secret had been given him by Orunmila, the deity of divination and the eldest son of Olodumare, and he had no authority to pass it on. He built a forge, and since he was both warrior and hunter he made hunting spears and knives as well as sharp, unbending swords.

The other *orishas* watched him come and go, bringing home his catches. Finally they offered to accept him as their king if he would share with them the secret of ironmaking. Ogun agreed and in time the knowledge spread to all the neighboring kingdoms and to all people on Earth.

Walukaga's Impossible Task

Once, a king of the Baganda people, in what is now Uganda, tested the skill of his blacksmith Walukaga by asking him to go beyond the limits of his craft. The genre of story in which a powerful ruler sets one of his subordinates an impossible task is familiar from many cultures.

The king wanted to make all men regard his territory with awe. He summoned his smith Walukaga and ordered him to make a man of flesh and blood out of iron. Now it was well known that the king would fly into a fury when crossed, so the renowned Walukaga did not demur. But he was troubled, for he saw that this task was beyond him, but that the king would be angry if he did not attempt it.

When he asked his friends for advice, none could help him—save one, a man to whom he had been close but who had since been dismissed as mad. This fellow suggested that Walukaga should agree to take on the task—but only if certain preconditions were met. The king should command his subjects to shave their heads and burn their hair to create 1,000 loads of charcoal with which to fire the furnace. He should also order them to collect their tears to make 100 pots of water to pour on the fire and prevent the forge overheating.

Walukaga asked and the king issued the orders. But the tribesmen could not do as commanded—their burnt hair provided only a single load of charcoal, and their tears just two pots of water. Then the king summoned Walukaga and announced that he was freed from his onerous task because the charcoal and water could not be found. Walukaga thanked his monarch and said that he had set impossible preconditions to the job because the king had asked him to perform an impossible task. The king laughed and Walukaga's wisdom was praised far and wide.

93

Anarchic First Man

The Bapedi and Bavenda, Bantu tribes from Transvaal in South Africa, recount that the first human, Huveane the shepherd, was a lawless trickster who loved to make mischief.

Huveane cared for his father's goats and sheep—for although he was the first man he had parents. One day, he set about making a being of his own: he took some clay, formed a baby with it, and then breathed life into it. Then he hid the baby near his parents' house. He cared for it lovingly, creeping out each dawn to feed it, but his parents noticed the dwindling supply of milk. Curious, Huveane's father followed him one day and saw the child. Taking it in his arms, he hid it beneath the house with the firewood. That evening Huveane discovered that his precious creation was missing; distraught, he slumped glumly with his parents at the fire. Distressed by his low spirits, his mother asked him to fetch some logs, whereupon he discovered the unharmed baby and capered with joy. His parents were so pleased to see him happy again that they allowed him to keep it.

On another occasion, Huveane played games with the herds. Each time a goat or ewe gave birth to twins, he stole one and hid it in an ant-heap. But one day a family friend told his father that he had seen the sheep and goats gathering around the ant-heaps. He followed his son there and discovered an entire young flock. He set them free and they ran in a frenzied whirl around the two men, calling for their mothers. That evening neighbors were struck dumb with astonishment and envy when they saw the size of the flock being driven home, for the recovered creatures had swelled it to almost twice its former size.

Huveane Escapes Death

The villagers began to gossip about Huveane, and before long they had decided that he was a danger who used evil magic. They even persuaded his own parents that he might bring ruin on them all.

Reluctantly, the couple decided he must die. First his mother gave him a poisoned bowl of milk, but he poured the harmful liquid straight into the dust without even examining it. Next his father dug a pit and covered it with matting to make a trap. But that night Huveane sat in an unusual place among his brothers and there was much pushing and shoving—in the course of which one of the others fell into the trap. A hole was dug on the path he took home in the evenings, but he and his flock simply jumped over it.

A villager then volunteered to attack Huveane, hidden inside a bale of grass. Huveane's father sent his son to bring in the bale, but Huveane inexplicably took his own spear and hurled it. The man within fled for his life; Huveane returned and told his father that the grass had run away.

The villagers concluded that they would have to learn to live with the crafty Huveane. It was not easy, however, for he plagued them and his family with a series of practical jokes. Out hunting with his father one day, the two men grew thirsty. Huveane pointed out a pool of cool water hidden high up in the rocks and helped his parent climb to it by knocking pegs into the rock-face. But once his companion was at the top drinking, Huveane slipped away, taking the pegs with him. Then he ran home and ate a vast meal, leaving none for anyone else. He filled the cooking pot with dung, then rescued his father and brought him back for a choice meal.

In some accounts Huveane appears to be identified with the maker of all things. Huveane means "Son of Huve," and some San prayed to a deity named Uwe or Huwe, said to be the creator of wild things. Among southern Africa's Basuto, Huveane is the name of the sky god whose exploits echo in the Huveane tales.

Huveane, the ancient South African trickster, was believed, like a divine creator, to have fashioned his own baby from clay. One of seven Lydenburg Heads from Transvaal, c.500–700 CE, this mysterious, primeval visage was made from clay and has traces of white pigment. It was probably used in a ritual.

Unwitting Agents of Order

Among the myriad tales about tricksters is a group that explains the conditions of everyday life. In these tricksters are, through their mischief and their frequent conflict with the great sky gods, the source of many things, good and bad, in the world. In some tales, a side effect of the tricksters' lawlessness is the creation of social order.

The antics of Ananse, the mischievous trickster spider of the Ashanti of Ghana and other Akan peoples, give rise to many familiar aspects of life, from disease to the presence of the sun and moon in the sky. Diseases first came among the Akan tribes in the following way. Once Ananse visited the sky god Nyame and asked to be given a choice sheep on which to feast; in return he promised to bring a tall, sleek-skinned maiden for Nyame's pleasure. Nyame agreed, but Ananse did not keep his side of the bargain.

He took the sheep to a village he knew where no menfolk but many beautiful maidens lived, and threw a great feast. Then, far from selecting any of the women for Nyame, Ananse married the entire population and satisfied his lust with them. A day came when a hunter who had passed through the village and seen Ananse indulging himself told Nyame what Ananse had done; the sky god dispatched messengers to the village to bring all the women to his domain. They did as they were told, save that they left one sickly woman with Ananse.

Now Ananse was in low spirits and he wondered aloud what he could do. The woman stirred; she told him to fetch a gourd, to wash her in water, and then pour the used water into the container. When Ananse did this she became a fine beauty and he rejoiced at his good fortune. The hunter, passing through, saw the beauty and told the sky god that Ananse had kept the most desirable of all

The blackness of this Akan *akuaba* doll represents night as the period of spiritual power. The sky god Nyame created night only because Ananse told him of the people's need for rest.

the women for himself. Nyame sent messengers to summon her to his presence. When they arrived Ananse took the gourd, stretched an elephant hide over it, and used it as a drum, setting up a subtle rhythm to which he danced. The messengers told Nyame of the dance and he summoned Ananse and his wife to show him.

In the presence of Nyame, Ananse played the gourd drum and Nyame danced with all his many, many wives. Ananse's remaining wife would not dance, however, because she knew the gourd-drum contained diseased water. The sky god, seeing this, grew angry—and forced her to do so. Then Ananse struck his wife with the gourd and the hide split. The diseases flew everywhere and they have plagued the Akan peoples ever since.

The Gifts of Ananse and Ture

In one cycle of stories, Ananse took the petitions of hard-pressed humans up to the sky god. In the deep past, it is said, men and women had to work in the fields without a break, for there was no darkness in which to rest. Ananse spun a thread to Heaven and told Nyame of the despairing pleas of the people in the fields. In response, Nyame created night so that people could rest. But the people were frightened of the newly arrived dark. Once again, Ananse informed Nyame; then the sky god set the moon in the arch of Heaven.

In the grey light of the fields men and women shivered and begged for warmth; Ananse brought this latest prayer to Nyame, who made the burning sun. Then the sun was too hot and on the people's behalf Ananse begged Nyame for respite; he sent the cooling rains. The waters fell and fell, creating floods that drowned the unwary; when Ananse told him of this, Nyame made the courses of the rivers and the deep bed of the sea to restrain their flow. Finally, people complained that even beneath the

rainclouds it was too hot, and the great and merciful Nyame sent a cooling wind to relieve them.

Ture was the spider trickster of the Zande, a group of Central African peoples who inhabit an area encompassing parts of Sudan, the Central African Republic, and Congo. Like Ananse, he brought many good things to his people. At one time only one man in the world had food, and all the others died of starvation. Ture pretended he wanted to make a blood pact of brotherhood with the man, who as a result showed him the place in the sky where he found his food. Ture brought it down and handed it out to the others. There was also a woman who kept all the water dammed up for herself and liked to slit the throats of people who were choking on food because they had nothing to drink. Ture stole a little water in a gourd so that when she cooked yams for him he would not choke. But he pretended to choke anyway, then slipped away from her, broke the dam, and set the waters free.

Ananse petitioned Nyame to bring rain to relieve people working in the glaring heat of the sun. Rain clouds build up over the jacaranda trees of the African plain.

Ananse, Owner of Stories

In a well-known story, Ananse used his cunning to force Nyame to give him ownership of all the stories told in the world. The spider first boldly asked Nyame if he could buy the stories from him. Nyame declared himself willing to part with them, but set what he thought was an impossible precondition: Ananse must deliver to him the hornets, the python, and the leopard.

Ananse went calmly about the task. He drilled a hole in a gourd, then filled a calabash with water. He went to the hornets' tree and wet both himself and them. Then he pretended that a storm was raging and suggested that they fly into the safety of the dry gourd. They did as he suggested and he filled

Ananse tricked the hornets into his gourd, then sealed it with grass and took it to Nyame in response to the god's challenge.

the gourd's hole with grass so that they could not escape. He then delivered them to Nyame.

Next Ananse went with a long staff and some vines to find the python. He told the snake that he had argued with his wife over whether the mighty python was shorter or longer than this great staff; at once the python offered to compare lengths. Ananse said that it looked as if the serpent were shorter but he could not be absolutely sure unless he first tied the python's head to the staff. The python, desperate to prove itself, acquiesced. Once he had tied the head, Ananse was able to tie the python's tail to the other end of the pole. He delivered him to Nyame.

Finally Ananse made a deep hole in the jungle in the place where the leopard roamed and disguised it with branches. The leopard fell in and Ananse persuaded him that his only hope of escape was for Ananse to bend a tall tree and tie the cat's tail to its top; when Ananse released the tree it would lift him to safety. The leopard agreed, Ananse released the tree and the leopard instead found himself hanging high above the ground. It was easy for Ananse to kill the beast and take him to Nyame. Astonished by Ananse's success, Nyame honored his promise and gave the spider control of the stories.

Nyame Gives the Sun First Place

Another story explained why evil actions usually take place in darkness and why children scamper at play beneath the moon. It told how Nyame gave issue to three offspring: Owia (Sun), Osrane (Moon) and Esum (Darkness), but he loved Owia best of all. Nyame made a stool that he intended to present to his best-loved as a sign of favor. He declared that none present could read his mind and all agreed, save argumentative Ananse. But later Ananse was worried, for he knew that if he were forced to prove his claim he would be unable to do so.

As night fell Ananse crept into

Nyame's garden and hid: in the cool dark he overheard the sky god speaking aloud, saying that he would hold a contest between his offspring to see who could remember the name of a particular yam: Kintinkyi.

Ananse brought the three children to Nyame. On the way he took Owia aside and told him what he had overheard. He said that he would play a rhythm on a little drum that would remind Owia of the name. All went exactly as planned and Nyame was greatly pleased when Owia won the contest. Ananse spun hither and thither in his joy. Nyame declared that Esum, who had not remembered the name, would witness evil deeds in the darkness of night for evermore; and Osrane, who had also forgotten, would see nothing more significant than young children at their innocent games in the moonlight. But Owia would be made chief of his brothers, although he was the youngest, and be granted the royal stool. In the clear light of day people on Earth would gather to settle disputes over important matters.

Another group of stories explains why Ananse is a spider. One claims that he was originally a man, but he aroused the anger of a king by killing one of his sheep. Outraged, the ruler kicked him so hard that he burst into innumerable pieces that flew throughout the kingdom taking on the form of spiders, which have ever since been ubiquitous. It was also maintained that spiders hide away in long grass or in shady corners because Ananse, their prototype, was often caught out in his deceptions and was so embarrassed that he fled to a place where he could not be seen.

Order from Disorder

Sometimes the fractious behavior of the trickster even helped create order. In a tale about Legba, divine trickster of the Fon (see pages 104–107), the unruly lover of quarrels is the unlikely source of a tradition designed to settle disputes.

In this story Legba was the youngest of three siblings—the eldest was Minona, a girl, the middle one Aovi, a boy. They traveled to play music at the

funeral of an important man (see page 105), where they performed so skilfully that at the end of the ceremony they were well paid in cowrie shells.

Outside the town they sat down at a crossroads and began to share out the shells. But there was an uneven number and they quarreled over the odd shell, although it was virtually worthless. They hailed a woman as she hurried past and forced her to count out the shells. Again there was one left over. The woman claimed there was no difficulty, for in such cases it was traditional to give the odd one to the eldest of the group, so Minona should have it. In fury, Aovi chopped off the woman's head. They hid her body in the bush and asked another passerby. The second unfortunate suggested giving the extra shell to the middle sibling, and at once Minona killed her. A third person was dispatched by both Minona and Aovi when she suggested giving the shell to the youngest. Finally Legba took himself off into the bush. He had the sack of his master Fa, the figurehead for the Fon cult of divination; in it he found a carving that he transformed into a lithe, long-legged dog. Legba and his creature ran back to the crossroads. There the dog solved the difficulty, for he took the odd shell and buried it, saying that from now it would be traditional in such cases to offer the extra amount to the tribal ancestors. Later when his siblings were not looking, Legba turned the dog back to wood and slipped it back into Fa's sack. It was to save him when he stood accused of the three murders (see page 106).

The traditional African currency of cowrie shells feature on this ancestral doll from Cameroon's Bamun people.

Keen Wits of Ananse

Ananse's endless cunning was put to effective use in outwitting an obstinate man and in a seemingly hopeless conflict with the mighty elephant.

Ananse heard that a man who lived by himself in a lonely forest clearing had killed several animals simply because they argued with him. The man's name was Hates To Be Contradicted and he would never let himself be bested in an argument. Ananse set off on foot to confront the recluse.

When he first arrived the two sat together sociably enough. Many ripe palm nuts fell from the hermit's tree and Hates To Be Contradicted launched into a nonsensical explanation of his nuts and his tree. He said that the nuts always ripened three bunches at a time, and that then he boiled them to make three pots of oil, which he took to the market. He exchanged them there for an old woman and when she returned to the clearing with him it was to give birth to his own grandmother. Then the grandmother gave birth to his mother and when his mother gave birth to him he stood idly by and watched. Ananse nodded seriously and replied that the explanation was perfectly reasonable. He countered with a description of his farm where, he said, he grew okra. When it was time to pick the crop, Ananse said, he tied seventy-seven poles together, but still could not reach the okra. So he was forced to pick the crop through other fantastical means. Hates To Be Contradicted nodded thoughtfully and promised to come and see.

Ananse went home to his village. He warned his children that a man was coming who would not be contradicted. Hates To Be Contradicted followed Ananse's tracks to the village and found his way to the trickster's home. The children greeted him.

Ananse then appeared to greet his guest. He asked the children to cook for the man, and they produced a fierce dish spiced with hot peppers.

Hates To Be Contradicted gasped for water but the children patiently explained that different levels of water in the pot belonged to different family members: at the top it belonged to Ananse, beneath that it was the property of Ananse's second wife, and at the bottom was the water of their mother, Ananse's first wife. They would like, they said, to give him some of the water that belonged to their mother but they could see no way of pouring it out without mixing up all the water, which would cause a terrible family argument.

Now Hates To Be Contradicted, whose throat was on fire from the peppers, fairly yelled that it was a lie. Ananse at once commanded his children to beat their guest to death. When the man complained, Ananse declared that although the man would not accept contradiction himself he had tried to contradict others; so he must die. Ananse's children enacted their father's desire. Then Ananse chopped up the man's carcass and flung its parts hither and thither. So argumentativeness and contradiction settled in the world to plague the tribes of the Akan kingdoms—and other peoples as far as the wide horizon.

Spider Takes on Elephant

In his contest with the towering elephant, Ananse demonstrated his cunning and capacity to deceive. On a long day time dragged for the elephant and he trumpeted a challenge for any creature to compete with him in a head-butting contest. All the animals saw it would mean certain death, save Ananse for whom nothing was impossible. With the elephant he agreed that their contest would run for fourteen nights; the elephant would have his seven butts over the first seven and then Ananse would respond.

It was a time of famine, but Ananse as ever had his own supplies; his plan was fully formed in his head and he put it into action. First he cooked some yams, then he went to sit in the latrine. He waited until an antelope was passing then threw a discarded tuber down on the path outside as if he had just used it to wipe himself. The antelope stopped, amazed that in a time of famine Ananse had excess food to use in this way. Ananse inveigled him into his house with the promise of food and then spun a tall tale about a man who brought him supplies by night. Ananse said that the antelope could have a share of them if he waited up for the delivery, and of course the antelope was keen to play a part. Ananse gave him detailed instructions. When the man came in the darkness, the antelope was to offer to receive his gift on his head.

So that night, when the elephant came in darkness for the first round of the head-butting, it was the antelope who offered his head and who received the full force of the elephant's strength. The antelope died; when Ananse rose in the morning he took the beast and gave it to his wife to make a rich stew. Over the six nights that followed, he tricked six more animals into

taking his place in the butting contest. Each one became meat for Ananse's own pot.

Then the night came on which Ananse was to hit back at the elephant. He set off for the beast's dwelling carrying an iron hammer and wedge, and when the elephant presented his head to him he drove the wedge deep into it. The elephant complained of a headache, but did not fall down. On the second night though, when Ananse drove in a second wedge, the elephant collapsed, never to rise again.

Ananse's cunning intelligence proved more than a match for the elephant's overwhelming size and power when he managed to kill it in a head-butting contest, the outcome of which might otherwise have seemed a foregone conclusion. Ashanti gold pendant bearing an elephant motif.

Hlakanyana the Zulu Trickster

Zulu tribes tell tales of a miniature trickster who took the name Hlakanyana and was linked to the weasel. No creature, human or animal, could match him for natural intelligence and animal cunning.

Hlakanyana is one of many figures in African mythology and folklore to have emerged from his mother's womb fully formed and with remarkable abilities. Even before he was born he could speak, and he called out impatiently demanding exit. On the very day of his birth he walked into the cattle kraal, ate some roasted flesh, outwitted some men in a race for a side of meat, and then took all the winnings home to his mother. His first night on Earth he slept in the *ilau* or boys' house with much older boys, despite their objections.

These colorful earplugs were given to Zulu girls at puberty. Hlankanyana bypassed the normal social ritual stages from childhood to adulthood, emerging fully mature from the womb.

He also played a trick on his mother reminiscent of that played by Huveane on his father (see page 94). First he took several birds from traps set by other boys and gave them to his mother to cook. The following morning, he rose very early and ate the birds out of the cooking pots, leaving only the heads. He filled up the pots with cattle dung and placed the birds' head on top. Then, at the normal time for rising, he returned to the hut. Now he pretended that it was late and complained that by sleeping so long his mother had allowed their food to spoil. He insisted that, because she had not taken the birds from their pots before sunrise, they would have turned to dung. The woman laughed, but he had only to lift the lids off the pots to silence her.

Then in the morning sunlight Hlakanyana took a stick and left his father's village. Hunger began to trouble him at about the time he came across some birds caught in traps. He stopped to take advantage of his good fortune, but the tracks were limed and he found he was caught fast. Then the wicked ogre who had set them sidled up and seized Hlakanyana. Eyeing up his plump and tender young catch, the giant drooled in cannibalistic delectation. But Hlakanyana with weasel words persuaded his dim-witted captor not to kill him there and then but to take him home to his mother, so that she could cook him.

In the ogre's cottage, Hlakanyana was left alone with the mother after the ogre and his brother went out on business. He tricked her into climbing into a pot, then boiled her alive. He donned her clothes and when the ogre and his brother came back, pretended to be the mother and told them to sit down to eat. While they were busy over their meat he ran away as fast as he could, pausing only to shout to them that they were eating their own mother. Driven by grief and dull rage they gave chase, but Hlakanyana was far too quick for the lumbering creatures.

The Hole and the Cubs

Another day he caused some simple mischief by stealing an old man's bread and scampering away. The poor fellow ran after Hlakanyana and saw him disappear into a snake's hole. Reaching an arm down into the darkness, he grabbed Hlakanyana around the ankle. But Hlakanyana only laughed and told the man that what he was holding was a tree root. The old man let go and at his next attempt really did seize a root. Now Hlakanyana cried aloud and said he would die if the man did not let go. The man grasped all the more tightly, but was left tugging fruitlessly at the root while inside Hlakanyana, smirking in the gloom, made short work of his bread. Later the man gave up and went away and Hlakanyana was able to slither out and go about his mischievous business.

In his next encounter Hlakanyana outwitted a mother leopard and her four cubs. He came among the cubs while the mother was out hunting, and when she returned, dragging the carcass of an antelope, she prepared to attack him. But his silky tongue did not fail him and he was able to persuade her to allow him to care for her cubs while she went hunting all the long day. As an inducement, he promised to build a thatched Zulu warrior's hut that would serve to shelter her and her family. While she was out the next day he made the hut and then ate one of the cubs. When she returned he brought the three surviving cubs out from the hut one at a time for her to suckle and then, in place of the fourth, brought out the first cub again. The following day he ate another cub and used the same trick to hide the fact from the mother. On the third evening, when there was only one cub left, he carried it out four times to be fed and at last it did not want any more. Then the mother became suspicious, but Hlakanyana told her the cub was sick and she was satisfied. Later he killed the leopardess, too. Finally Hlakanyana returned home, where his mother was completely overjoyed to see him.

He died young and in a very curious manner. One day when he was watching over his father's flock he encountered a tortoise and took it home on his back. When his mother came to lift it off she could not, for the tortoise was frightened and clung on tightly. Hastily she poured some hot liquid over the tortoise and the animal let go, but the liquid also scalded Hlakanyana and brought him to a premature end.

Traditional Zulu storytellers say that Hlakanyana is like a weasel, filled with cunning. Scholars believe it likely that in the oldest myths, Hlankanyana actually was a weasel and that in the shape of an animal he was infused with divine powers. Many of his exploits have parallels in the hare stories (see pages 108–109), possibly reflecting the common cultural heritage of the Bantu-speaking peoples.

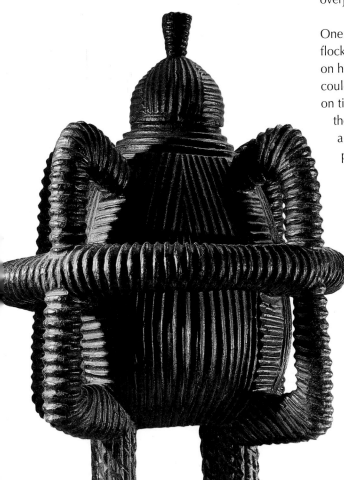

Many of the Hlakanyana stories are concerned with food. Carved, lidded vessels were used in parts of southern Africa as milk pails or to hold roasted meat.

Legba the Lecher God

The lawless, voracious trickster Legba recognized by the Fon of Dahomey was the youngest, spoiled son of the creator deity Mawu-Lisa. Myths of his exploits celebrate his strength and virility as well as his intelligence.

Legba stayed with his mother-father when the other gods moved into their kingdoms, and because they developed different languages he became their interpreter, the linguist of the gods. None of the divinities—and far less any human worshippers—can address Mawu-Lisa without going through Legba. But he cannot be trusted, for he is the soul of random action and loves to stir up dissension. He often disobeys his master Fa, personification of the Fon divination cult, and undermines his authority. Legba is everywhere and cannot be caught—he is an elusive, invisible spirit found at crossroads and in doorways and open spaces in front of houses.

The Fon say that Legba is the gods' chief as well as their interpreter. He was the youngest and had no authority with his siblings, but one time Mawu-Lisa produced four musical instruments—flute, drum, bell, and gong—and announced that the one among them who could play all four instruments while dancing would become their chief. Now all the gods were full of pride and were eager to prove their ability. But one after another they failed. Then Legba sidled up, and before the others knew it he had all the instruments in his hands and was playing them together, while twisting and gesturing in the dance. Mawu-Lisa was delighted that her youngest had won the contest and made him chief. She fashioned him a wife named Konikoni.

Legba knew many mysterious things and he had the power of magic. In high spirits, he slipped down to Earth to make charms. First he made a serpent and set it loose in a marketplace. When it bit the traders he appeared and offered to cure them if they gave him food and drink. That night he ate a large meal washed down with palm wine.

One man, named Awe, watched Legba's comings and goings and saw the power of his magic. He asked Legba for the secret and in return for chickens, straw, and a good quantity of cowrie

Fa, the Fon ruler of divination, could not speak without Legba's help. This 19th-century Fon silver lion represents one of their king's divination signs, his name meaning "Lion of Lions."

shells, Legba duly passed on his knowledge. From that time Awe became known for his magic, although in truth it all came from Legba.

This act made Mawu-Lisa angry with her favorite and she summoned Legba to Heaven. She turned her son invisible, declaring that this might stop him from exploiting his magic. Ever since, he has walked as unseen as the other gods, who are clothed only in air. Awe now had the power of magic and was celebrated far and wide, but he used his charms to cause mischief as well as to cure and help people.

Guardian of Gods and Men

When Legba attended the funeral with Minona and Aovi (see page 99), he also performed a service for his master Fa—the ruler of divination, who cannot speak without Legba's assistance. Fa was approached by the son of a minor monarch, the king of Adja. The great King Metonofi, first king on Earth, ruler without equals, had given his daughter to the king of Adja, but the marriage had never been consummated. Shame hung over the royal house so the king passed the maiden on to his son. Now the son was concerned that he too might fail to prove the virility of his clan and he wanted Fa to help him to father a child with the help of a special powder.

Fa wanted to dispatch a powder to the palace at Adja, but Legba intervened, insisting that he had the powders at his side in Fa's sack and asking permission to dispense some there and then. Fa acquiesced, so Legba took the king's son aside to begin his mischief. In the bag were two powders: one, red in color, made men powerless; the other, which was white, restored their powers. Legba gave the young man a dose of the red powder. The poor deceived young man went away anticipating joy on his homecoming.

Legba's interference meant that the son of the king was no more able to father a child with the princess than his father had been. Then the girl's father, King Metonofi, proclaimed that whoever could father a child with her would win half of his kingdom. Ambitious men flocked from all corners of the kingdom to consult Fa, but they had to address Legba and the trickster made them all powerless by giving them the red powder. When the king discovered who was behind the trouble, he sent soldiers to arrest Legba. But he had gone into hiding at his mother-in-law's house. He was a typical, taboo-breaking trickster, heedless of consequences.

105

Eshu

Legba's equivalent among the Yoruba is the divine messenger Eshu. In a celebrated exploit, Eshu tore apart a harmonious friendship and brought chaos to a town.

Two men had been friends since they were boys and appeared to agree in all things. They farmed adjacent fields, sowing the same crops at the same time, and even shared a taste in clothes. But Eshu came between them.

One day he set off walking along the path that divided the friends' fields. He wore a multi-colored, red and white hat. He placed his pipe so it seemed to be coming out of the back of his neck instead of his mouth and hung his walking stick over his deep shoulders instead of his chest. The two men, bent over the work, saw Eshu pass and when they straightened up to rest their backs they began to quarrel about the color of the trickster's hat and the direction in which he had been walking. At length words failed them and they began to trade blows. Finally they were dragged before the king.

Eshu came into the royal presence just as the two men were explaining themselves, and he confessed that he had set up the quarrel because of his love of mischief. The king ordered Eshu's arrest, but the trickster had already taken flight and could not be caught. He ran through the town spreading panic by setting fire to the buildings he passed. As the people ran out of their houses trying to save their possessions, Eshu offered to look after the precious bundles. But he muddled the parcels up so that a dispute began. At this point laughing Eshu took his leave.

Legba Faces Trial

The following day Legba was arrested and hauled into the presence of King Metonofi to be judged. First he stood accused of the murder of the three women at the crossroads (see page 99). But he truthfully replied that he had killed none of the three, for Minona and Aovi had struck the blows; he also stated that he had made a dog whose wise counsel had solved the quarrel. To prove it, he took the wooden model from Fa's sack of resources and changed it again into living flesh.

The audience gasped and saw that on this rare occasion Legba spoke the truth. Metonofi decreed that the trickster should become guardian of men and gods. He said that Minona should live in women's houses and be their protector. Aovi should be an air-clothed divinity and live with the gods. Legba could come and go as he chose.

Next Legba was judged on the charge that he had had an affair. For this misdeed he was to be permitted only to dwell on the ground in front of people's houses.

Legba also faced a third trial. He was accused of deliberately giving the men of the kingdom a drug. In this case cunning came to his rescue. Using pigeon blood, he dyed the white powder red, and by adding water made the red powder white. When Metonofi asked his subjects which color powder Legba had given them, they declared that it had been the red one. Now Legba happily agreed to a trial in which he himself would take the red powder and see if it had the same effect.

Legba publicly swallowed some of the red powder, which the onlookers expected would make him powerless. He ordered drums to be played and went in to the princess. Then, while the drums still pounded, Legba came strutting out of the house in triumph.

Metonofi yelled his approval. He ordered that the playing of the drums should become a custom in the tribe, and said that Legba could choose any woman he desired. Legba in return decreed that Metonofi should become ruler of the dead and guardian of the threshold between the worlds of living and dead. Legba did not take Metonofi's daughter as his wife, but passed her on to Fa. The ruler of divination held a grand wedding ceremony, at which Legba slipped the powder into the jugs of palm wine. That night all the men present rejoiced.

Neighboring Eshu

Legba's character and role are mirrored by Eshu, the divine trickster of the Yoruba, near-neighbors of the Fon (see box opposite). Both are go-betweens from humans to the masters of divination. Eshu rides the shifting wind of impulse, seizing every opportunity to overturn rules and stir up the status quo. Also like Legba, Eshu is the gods' interpreter and linguist, and stories celebrating his conquests match those of Legba.

Eshu, like Legba, carries messages to the great sky god, and offerings must be made to him prior to divination. The row of calabash gourds on his headdress signal his supernatural powers. Long cowrie shell braids recall his prominent role in trade; his principal shrine was usually in the marketplace. Yoruba figure, 19th century.

107

The Outwitting of the Mischief-Maker

Among the Bantu-speaking peoples, the trickster adventures of the untrustworthy hare and the resourceful tortoise are recounted with much glee. Peoples from all over southern, eastern, and central Africa share a delight in the tradition.

A widespread story tells how the hare—as ever wanting something for nothing—was seeking a way of making someone else perform the hard work of clearing a field so that he could plant some millet. He took a rope and scampered into the bush until he saw the great bottom of a hippopotamus looming out of the dusty atmosphere. The sweet-tongued hare persuaded the hippopotamus to tie the rope around its neck, pretending he wanted to play tug-of-war. He told the hippopotamus to pull with all his might as soon as he felt a tug on the rope. Then off skipped the hare, with the rope's other end gripped between his teeth. He sought out an elephant and tricked him in the same way. When the hare gave the rope a tug, both the elephant and the hippopotamus pulled as hard as they could. As they strained with all their might they trampled backward and forward over the bush, clearing a wide area of vegetation. The hare then sauntered up to plant his millet.

Tortoise Outwits Hare

One popular tale recounts how the hare at last met his match and was caught out by the wily tortoise. It was at a time of terrible drought when the fierce ball of the sun followed the animals everywhere like a divine hunter from whom there was no escape. The kingly lion ordered all the animals to assemble on a riverbed that had dried to a hard sur-face. All came, save the hare who said he could not be bothered.

The lion then instructed each animal to stamp on the dry riverbed in an attempt to draw water out of it. They tried one by one, but with no success. Finally the humble tortoise stepped forward. He trod on the ground and it grew softer, trod again and the ground grew damp. The rhinoceros could watch no more, for he felt keenly the shame of having been outperformed by a mere tortoise.

A cult mask with a human face adorned with the figures of two lizards and a tortoise. The latter never gets defeated in tales.

Maddened by the sun, he charged and flipped the tortoise with his strong horn. The tortoise smashed against a rock and his shell broke into pieces. The rhinoceros tried stamping on the ground where the tortoise had been, but as he did so he only raised more dust and the dampness quickly evaporated.

The tortoise patiently pieced his shell together and when the other animals asked him to come and try again he was ready to do so. As soon as he began, the ground grew wet. Before long water was flowing, and it filled a deep well that the animals had prepared.

The animals' troubles seemed to be over, but one thing bothered them—for they guessed that the hare would soon try to steal their water despite the fact that he had made no effort to conjure it from the ground. They agreed to stand guard over it all through the night. First on duty was the hyena. As expected, as soon as darkness fell there came the light footfall of the hare, who scampered up carrying two calabashes, one full of honey and one empty. Now the hare pretended that the honey he carried was sweet water and tempted the hyena away from the well to taste a little of it. Then he promised the hyena a good draught, but insisted he had first to tie him to a tree because the water was so sweet it would otherwise knock him over. In his foolishness, the hyena accepted the condition. As soon as the beast was safely tied up, the hare leaped up to the well, drank deeply, gargled to soothe his throat, and even had a long leisurely swim.

The next night the lion was caught out by the same trick and on the nights that followed a succession of other animals fell victim to the hare's sweet tongue. Finally only the tortoise was left. Now the tortoise planned his night watch carefully. First he rolled in birdlime so that his shell was quite covered, then he jumped into the deep well and hid beneath the water. When the hare skipped up at midnight he found the well unguarded and assumed the animals had given up trying to keep him away. After drinking and resting, he stepped in for his bath. Both his hindfeet stuck on the tortoise's lime-covered shell. The hare put down first one foreleg and then the other until all four legs were stuck to the tortoise's shell. There was no escape, and through the long hours of darkness he remained there, glued to his captor, awaiting a humiliating dawn.

The other animals, finding the hare bested for once, scampered and skipped with delight. They decided to tie him up as punishment, but the hare put his facility with words to good use again. He pretended to accept that he had done wrong and even that he must die; but he begged that when they tied him in the beating sunshine and left him to perish they would use banana fiber rather than any other rope. The animals were persuaded. After some time exposed to the heat of the sun the fibres dried out and the hare was able to snap them. At liberty again, he skipped away before his captors could stop him.

The powerful rhinoceros was embarrassed at not being able to achieve what the tortoise managed to do so easily. It has remained, however, a symbol of strength and stability. Wooden headrest, East Africa.

Dark Spirits of the Forest Fastnesses

In many parts of the African continent, people tell tales of encounters with little people or spirits who frequent the dark heart of the forest. Rivers and streams, too, are believed to have their own prophetic, sometimes violent guardians.

The Mongo-Nkundo of Congo tell of the man-eating *biloko*, sharp-toothed dwarves who wander the pathless wastes at the heart of the great forests of Central Africa. These fearsome creatures sprout grass on their bodies where hair should grow and live in the hollow trunks of dead trees. Leaves are their only clothes. Their mouths, which form a snout like a wild beast's, can open wide enough to swallow a human body whole. Their claws tear human skin as easily as a man can rip a dry leaf. But most terrifying of all are their spells, for—like Itonde (see page 88)—they carry magic bells, whose tinkling casts a paralyzing trance on all who are not protected by a fetish or charm bracelet.

One story tells of a wife whose love for her husband was so strong that she insisted on accompanying him on a hunting trip into the deep forest. Her husband built a hut for her and surrounded it with sharp stakes, then crept away to check the traps he had set for the elusive forest beasts. Almost before her husband's goodbye had died on the air, the woman heard a sweet tinkling of bells and a forlorn child's voice asking her to open the door of the hut. When she did so, there was one of the *biloko*, giving off a smell of rotting vegetation. The dwarf complained of hunger even while it rang its deadly bell. When the woman offered food it cried, saying that only human flesh would satisfy its deep craving. The poor woman could hear only the chimes and was in time persuaded to let the snuffling snout touch and taste her arm. The following morning the hardy hunter, weighed down with meat, returned happily to his makeshift home, but he found only a pile of

The Boat Mascot

By tradition among the Ngbandi of Congo, fishermen working on a stretch of river where a man had died would take along his son, who was said to have the power to keep danger at bay.

When a man drowned, the Ngbandi said, the stretch of water where he lost his life became his property and he was able to pass ownership on to his descendants. It was customary for the surviving son to visit the place and to make offerings in his father's honor. The water, imbued with his father's spirit, became part of his inheritance.

For this reason fishermen would ask the son to travel with them if they went fishing in the area, for they knew that his drowned father's spirit would watch over them. No harm could befall a boat in which he traveled.

Every river, stream, and pool had its own spirit in Ngbandi belief and sometimes a river spirit might reach out and attack

Rivers might have spirits that required offerings to guarantee a safe passage. Chobe River, Botswana.

humans. People said prayers and made offerings to avert such catastrophes and also to ask for good things. For example, the spirit of the Bogo River had the gift of fertility and the power to bring rich harvests to the land. Fishermen in the area around the small Limalo River made offerings to the river spirit to ensure a plentiful supply of fish.

gnawed and splintered bones where his wife had been. Many Bantu tribes tell similar stories of forest-haunting demons.

Stories circulate among the Yoruba of demon spirits who can turn themselves into beautiful maidens or broad-chested hunters to waylay unwary forest travelers. Sometimes they settle with humans and either sire or give birth to demonic offspring, who later in life become witches, magicians, or renowned hunters. Such tales clearly influenced the story of Lonkundo, the hero of the Mongo-Nkundo (see pages 86–87).

Forest Doctor

In some traditions the little people are benign. The Fon of Dahomey recount how it was from a tiny spirit-being named Aziza that they learned the arts of medicine. Deep in the forest a hunter paused to rest and heard a voice that seemed to issue from a mound of earth. The speaker, who was Aziza, knew that the huntsman's wife suffered from leprosy and offered him some leaves as a cure for the condition. Aziza promised that he would treat any invalids who needed healing, if the hunter would guide them to the spot. The hunter cured his wife with the leaves and later led the sick among his people to Aziza.

Some scholars suggest that the short-statured pygmies who now live only in the forests of Central Africa were once far more widely spread and that tales of the little people may derive from encounters between wandering tribesmen and pygmy hunters.

THE MYSTIQUE OF MASKS

Africa was, and is, home to thousands of cultures with distinct beliefs, customs, stories, and festivals. Countless ceremonies were performed, often requiring specific dress, such as masks, or involving ritualized dances or actions on the part of the participants. Together these formed powerfully recognizable displays of both ritual and tribal identity, and although religious traditions differed in intent the ceremonies were generally held to engender a positive relationship with the world of the spirits upon which depended the well-being of both individuals and the community at large.

Powerful energies were thought to exist that could act as sacred intermediaries between humans and gods, with powers to harm or protect. These go-betweens could be contacted through the use of masks and headdresses.

Headwear's central function was to represent and invoke the deities. By manifesting the spirit in the human world a mask might protect initiates from witches or give warriors power over their enemies.

The well-known *ci wara* animal headdresses of the Bamana farmers of Mali and the Ivory Coast are a very good example of spiritual-social crossover. The significance of masks varies between different Bamana groups, depending on who or what is using them, but they are always linked with agriculture, successful cultivation, and bountiful harvests. Spiritual forces need to be propitiated to ensure this outcome is achieved. The *ci wara* masks, however, simply celebrate and respect particular gods and animals that epitomize certain values associated with good farming practice.

Masked dances used to reflect essential beliefs of the culture, although today many have lost their religious significance and are now conducted primarily as a form of entertainment. One typical example is the *dama*, celebrated by the Dogon of Mali. The *dama* is a festival of life and death, a pageant of the Dogon universe, the life-forms that inhabit it, and the spirits presiding over it. The young, male dancers descend in single file into the village from the hills of their ancestors, led by one of their number wearing the *kanaga* mask of the creator while others sport masks representing aspects of God's human or animal creation. Bringing up the rear is the tall mask of the "many-storeyed house," symbolic of the ancestral serpent that led them to their cliff-face territory.

Far Left: Egungun Society mask made of painted wood and consisting of a variety of entwined beings. The figures probably had a topical significance, but more generally represented the life-sustaining power and continued existence of the Yoruba lineage. *Odun egungun*, or festivals for the ancestors, are celebrated throughout the Yoruba lands.

Left: This stilt dancer, attired in symbolic red, represents a spirit ancestor during the *dama* festival, reflecting a belief that the Dogon originated in a country of water herons. The performance is partly intended to attract a dead person's soul away from its old home and onward into the land of the spirits, where it will be free from its suspense and able to rest as a guardian of the people.

Above: Masked societies play an important role in the preservation of mythology. Here, at a ceremonial in Tireli, dancers reaffirm the Dogon's rightful claim to their homeland. These men probably represent *walu*, the strong and graceful antelope. Those who best reproduce the animal's elegant movements earn the audience's warmest appreciation.

Right: Coming-of-age initiations often culminate in a dance or a ritual of one kind or another. Masai warriors in Kenya participate in a colorful, male rite of passage that confirms the individual's and group identity as well as the continuity of the people and their traditions.

Left: A line of Dogon dancers wear masks representing various animals or hybrid creatures. For many mask-wearing festivities the participants must belong to a special society, usually male-only. The dancers serve to link the entire community with the spirit world or with the creatures they represent, although they themselves are not necessarily practicing magicians or possessed by supernatural forces.

Right: *Ci wara* dancers among the Bamana of West Africa wear stylized *dagwe* or antelope headdresses. The spirit who introduced the people to agriculture did so in the form of this wild animal of the bush.

Right: Dancers among the Kuba-speaking Bushoong people of Congo wear masks such as this *moshambwooy* when reenacting their mythic origins. It represents the founder figure Woot and also has strong associations with the world of water spirits or *ngesh* to whom the Bushoong diviners attribute their supernatural powers.

KINGDOMS AND EMPIRES

Every part of the world has well-preserved memories of the past, but in Africa they are particularly strong. In cultures where family ties were the dominant force and that for the most part were without writing, history was passed down orally from generation to generation. Under such circumstances, the narrator's urge to tell a story joined forces with the chronicler's desire to record events. Embroidered to hold an audience or to honor the mighty dead, the feats of famous ancestors turned easily into the stuff of legend.

There were many great deeds to recall. Scholars are only now coming to appreciate the size and wealth of the empires that flourished in Africa before the coming of Europeans. Precise origins are hard to ascertain, but from about the ninth century onward a chain of states developed in the so-called Sudanic lands south of the Sahara. Part of the impetus behind their growth came from contact with merchants from the Islamic states of North Africa, who bought gold, leatherwork, and slaves in return for salt and luxury goods.

Gold contributed much to the legends that developed externally about Africa in the Middle Ages. The earliest known West African empire was that of Ghana, established by the Soninke people from the eighth century onward in the area between the Senegal and Niger rivers. Other power centers developed later in the Yoruba city-states and the Hausa lands. Greatest of all, perhaps, was the empire of Mali, founded by the Mande people. When its ruler, Mansa Musa, went on pilgrimage to Mecca in 1324, he took so much gold with him that the currency of Egypt, where his retinue stayed en route, was depressed for years afterward.

Even older than the Sudanic states was the ancient kingdom of Ethiopia, which traced its history back to Menelik I, supposedly the son of the Queen of Sheba. Its Christian faith separated it from the Muslim city-states of the Swahili-speaking eastern coast, whose sultans grew rich on the Indian Ocean trade.

Most mysterious of all were the little-known kingdoms of the south. In the lands of the lake highlands and below the equatorial rainforest, Bantu-speakers came together in federations with rulers thought of as gods. And at Great Zimbabwe the Shona, enriched by gold exported through the port of Sofala, were raising the majestic stone enclosure that has puzzled observers for centuries and still impresses visitors today.

Opposite: Metal plaque showing the gateway to the palace of the *oba* of Benin, the great Edo kingdom of West Africa, c.17th century.

Below: Beaded stool from Cameroon. Many African peoples attached significance to stools; among the Ashanti, for example, a king's stool represented his authority over the Earth, on which it stood.

The Kings Who Came from the Sky

Myths from both sides of the continent told of gods who came down from the sky to people the Earth—and then stayed to create great kingdoms, including the artistically rich city-states of West Africa and the pastoralist realm of Buganda in the east.

The Yoruba people of southwestern Nigeria have one of Africa's finest artistic legacies, and their historical heritage is just as rich. Although most still make a living as farmers, they also have a long urban tradition, for Yoruba society developed in the form of a number of city-states, the best-known being Ile-Ife, Oyo, Owo, Ijebu, Ilorin, and Ibadan. Yoruba lived too in the great neigboring Edo city of Benin. In the cities themselves, the palace of the *oba* or king would be surrounded by the dwellings of shopkeepers, traders, and artisans, for the Yoruba were traditionally among the most skilled craftsmen on the continent, excelling in weaving, leather-work, glass-making, and ivory and wood carving.

Ile-Ife occupied a special place in Yoruba myth as the spot where the Earth was created (see pages 34–35). Oduduwa, who was sent down from the heavens to accomplish the task, went on to found the city itself. When the other *orishas*—the sky-dwelling gods of Yoruba legend—saw that his work was good, they came down to inspect it. One was Orunmila, who taught people the art of divination and founded the city of Benin.

The double-axe motif identifies this as a Yoruba Sango staff linked to the thunder and lightning *orisha*.

The Staff of Oranyan

In time the city's founder Oduduwa died, leaving the realm of Ile-Ife to his son Oranyan. The young man turned out to be an excellent ruler. He was a brave warrior and highly skilled in combat—a necessary pre-requisite, because warfare had come to Earth and the *obas* of other states looked enviously upon the might of Ile-Ife. Yet he remained undefeated, vanquishing every champion who came up against him and routing all the armies sent against the kingdom. As long as he lived, Ile-Ife was safe.

But old age crept up on Oranyan too. Knowing at last that death was near, he called the people together and told them to continue to resist all comers after he was gone. Grief swept the crowd at his words, and many voices were raised imploring him not to go. But he told them that was not possible. The most he could promise was to come back when danger threatened the city. He said that he would teach the elders of the city secret words by which they could summon him in time of need. And as a pledge of his word and an encouragement to future generations, he planted his wooden staff of office in the center of the marketplace. It turned miraculously into a column of stone and has stood there ever since, known as Oranyan's Staff to this day.

Oranyan was as good as his word. Upon news of his death, other powers sought to invade Ile-Ife to take advantage of his going. But when their armies approached the city, the elders spoke the secret words. With a noise like thunder the earth opened and the dead king stepped out, fully armed. The mere sight of his weapons flashing in the sun was

Bronzes from Benin

Some of Africa's most beautiful sculptures were created more than 500 years ago by craftsmen in the West African city-states of Ile-Ife and Benin.

Some of the works were made in terracotta—fired, unglazed clay—but others were so-called "bronzes" (actually the metal alloy was brass) produced by the lost-wax method. This technique, used by the Yoruba from about the eleventh century, involved covering a sculpted earthenware core with beeswax and an outer casing of clay. The beeswax was then melted out so the space left behind could be filled with molten metal.

The Ile-Ife sculptors' masterpieces were a series of life-size human heads, most probably portraits of rulers of the cities. They are thought to have been used in funerary rites, then either preserved for safe-keeping in the royal palaces or buried at marked spots in sacred groves. The most distinctive feature of the bronzes was their intense naturalism, rare not just in Africa but anywhere in the world at the time when they were produced. When the skills were passed on to Benin—according to tradition, by a famous craftsman named Igueghae late in the fourteenth century—a more stylized tradition developed.

A brass head of an Ile-Ife king, c.13th century. Most busts were produced for the royal court of the *oba*, who would dedicate an altar to his predecessor. Such figures were sometimes identified with Olukun, the Yoruba sea god and Benin's most worshipped deity.

119

enough to spread terror in the enemy ranks, which quickly broke and fled. Then Oranyan returned to the earth from which he had come and the ground closed once more over his regal head.

Word of his miraculous reappearance spread, and for many years Ile-Ife went unmolested. But in time security bred laziness and complacency. The people lost the sense of duty they had had in Oranyan's day and thought only of pleasure. One evening during festival time, when there was much dancing, drumming, and drinking of palm wine, some revelers drunkenly called on the elders to summon Oranyan to the celebrations. Shocked at such levity, they at first demurred, but the people insisted. Fearing for their own lives, the old men eventually gave in, summoning the great warrior with the ancient formula that told him that the city of Ile-Ife was in danger.

Oranyan appeared as before in a clap of thunder, gazing around for the foe. But because it was dark he could not tell one face from another. Seeing himself surrounded by what he took to be the enemy, he set about the bystanders, spearing many with his lance and cutting down others with his sword. Soon the marketplace was awash with blood, but the killing went on. Only when dawn broke and Oranyan could at last see the tribal scars on the faces of the dead did he realize that he had been slaughtering his own

Carved ivory cup for ritual and festive drinking, from Owo, c.15th century. The city-state of Owo was the ancient capital of the Yoruba. Bracelets and boxes were also carved from ivory tusks for the court.

people. Then he threw his weapons down in horror, and in anguished tones proclaimed that his fighting days were over. The earth closed around him, and from that day forth Oranyan was never seen in Ile-Ife again. Only his staff remained behind to remind succeeding generations of the city's greatest hero—and the foolish irreverence that had cost them his services for good.

The Trials of Kintu

One thousand eight hundred sixty-four miles (3,000 km) to the east, in Uganda, various peoples were united together by a story that traced another dynasty all the way back to a sky-being who decided to settle on Earth. This person was Kintu, first founder of the royal line of the *kabakas* (kings) of Buganda.

The stories told how Kintu at first had only a cow for company, and lived off the beast's milk. Then a pretty sky-maiden named Nambi saw him in his loneliness and fell in love with him. But when she told her family about him, they despised him as a mere milksop. To test him, they stole the cow, and for a time he had to grub a living from herbs and leaves.

Eventually Nambi came to tell Kintu that his animal had been taken up to Heaven, and he went with her to fetch it back. Nambi's father and brothers were waiting for him. They invited him into the mansion in which they lived, but not as a welcome guest. They planned to get rid of him by setting him an impossible task to perform on pain of his life. And so they presented him with a huge meal—enough to feed half a tribe—and told him to eat it all up or else he would be killed. He was left to get on with the task, but could barely digest one-tenth of the food provided. Then he noticed a half-hidden hole in the floor. Quickly he piled all the leavings into it and covered it over. When his hosts came back, they were astonished to find not a crumb remaining.

Nambi's father, Gulu, was not to be appeased so quickly, however, and he at once thought up another, equally daunting challenge. This time Kintu was given a copper axe and told to cut firewood from a rock. Once more he proved equal to the task, finding a boulder that was already deeply fissured and managing to strike splinters from it that he solemnly presented to his prospective father-in-law as fuel for his hearth. In return, he was handed a huge pot and told to fill it with water that came not from any river, lake, pond, or well. At a loss, he lay down in a field with the pot beside him—and was delighted to wake up early the next day to find it miraculously filled with morning dew.

By now Gulu was running out of ideas, but he thought he still had one winner up his sleeve. He told Kintu that he could indeed marry Nambi, but only if he could find the cow he had come to seek among his own extensive herds. This too seemed impossible, for Gulu was vastly wealthy and had countless cattle, many of them virtually identical to Kintu's beast. But once more Kintu triumphed, this time with the help of a friendly bumble bee, which promised to alight on the horns of the animal he was seeking.

So, when Kintu was taken out to the first of Gulu's herds the next morning, the first thing he looked for was the bee. He spotted it buzzing around in the shade of a tree, from which it refused to budge; so Kintu, getting the message, told Gulu that his cow was not among the cattle present. The same thing happened when Kintu visited a second herd. The third time, however, the bee at once flew to a large cow, and Kintu claimed it for his own.

Then it flew off again, only to settle in turn on three young calves. For a moment Kintu was nonplussed; then he had the presence of mind to insist that they too were his, having been born to his cow during her stay in Heaven.

Gulu was amazed. There seemed to be nothing that his daughter's suitor did not know. Convinced of his worthiness as a bridegroom, he finally gave his consent to the match. Married at last, the two returned to Earth to found the royal line of Buganda, which ruled the kingdom on the northern shores of Lake Victoria well into the twentieth century.

Reminiscent of the tool provided to Kintu, this elaborate copper-handled, iron-bladed axe was carried in a Central African ceremonial rite honoring the ancestors, who are possibly represented by the massed human heads.

121

The Vanishing City

The Soninke people of West Africa are spread across a wide area that covers modern Mali, Mauritania, and Senegal. They recall a great empire in tales of a disappearing city, lost four times through the folly of its citizens and rebuilt as often by their heroism.

Today the Soninke are mostly farmers, but they look back on an illustrious past as the founders of the ancient empire of Ghana, greatest of the pre-Islamic West African kingdoms. The realm, which was founded perhaps as early as the fourth century CE, prospered over the ensuing millennium, trading gold and ivory with Arab and Berber salt merchants from the north. The empire was known to its creators as Wagadu, and that is the name by which its capital is remembered by Soninke bards. In their tales it is not so much a real place as a state of mind. "For really," they say, "Wagadu is not of stone, not of wood, not of earth. Wagadu is the strength which lives in the hearts of men." And when that strength failed through the weakness or folly of its citizens, the city would vanish with it.

Four times Wagadu stood and four times it was lost. Should it ever reappear, the bards say, it will remain, for each visitation is more beautiful than the last, and the fifth "will live so forcefully in the minds of men that vanity, falsehood, greed and dissension will never be able to harm it."

There are whole cycles of stories about the city's incarnations, including the tale of Gassire's lute (see pages 82–83), which played a part in the first disappearance of the city. The best known concerns the city's second appearance, at the water-source of Kumbi—a real site tentatively identified as the capital of Ghana in the eleventh century—and its theme is that of a negotiated settlement to an inheritance dispute between siblings.

Kumbi was located by the Soninke chief Dinga's second son, Djabe Sisse, who had obtained the chieftainship by trickery (see box opposite). Dinga was old and wise; his magical powers had included understanding the language of animals, and he had revealed the secret of the Kumbi well to a vulture and a hyena, instructing them to direct his descendants there after his death, but warning them of a creature that would

After the Soninke fled Bida's city it is said that they founded Djenne. Terracotta rider and horse from Djenne, c.13th century.

Tricking Trikhinye

*Wagadu's second founder originally owed his preferment—
over his elder brother—to the guile of a mistreated servant.*

Under normal circumstances, Dinga's eldest son Trikhinye would have inherited the chieftainship of the tribe on the old ruler's death. But, as the bards tell the tale, he was cheated of his inheritance by a trick reminiscent of the one used by Jacob against his brother Esau in the Bible story.

In the Soninke version, the scheme was thought up by an old slave named Sitoure who had served Dinga faithfully for many years. Yet for all his loyalty, he had known nothing but abuse from Trikhinye, while the second son, Djabe Sisse, had always treated him kindly. So when the blind chief, close to death, asked for his eldest son to be brought to him for his blessing, Sitoure determined to fetch Djabe Sisse instead. But there was a problem—the younger son was smooth-skinned while the elder was rough and hairy.

Sitoure went to Djabe Sisse and explained the situation. He persuaded the young man to borrow his brother's jewelry— an armlet and a finger ring that Dinga always touched to recognize his eldest. Then he bound a piece of goatskin to the young man's arm before leading him into his father's presence.

Sightlessly, the old man reached for his son's arm and was reassured by what he felt. And so it came about that he passed on the secrets of the chieftaincy to Djabe Sisse and not to his elder brother, who had expected them as his birthright.

have to be placated. In time Djabe Sisse was informed and led his people to their destination, where they found a terrible surprise waiting.

A man-serpent named Bida lived in a deep well outside the city. It was actually an offspring of Dinga and therefore Djabe Sisse's half-brother. As "earth-owner" and controller of fertility, Bida required propitiation for allowing Djabe Sisse to rule politically and the tribe to settle. It agreed to settle annually for the best colt in the kingdom and the most beautiful maiden in the city. In return it guaranteed the prosperity of the community by causing a rain of gold to fall twice a year.

For many years the serpent received its victims and the city flourished. Then it came to the turn of Princess Siya Yatabere, whose cousin, Mamadi the Taciturn, vowed to save her. So he dug a hole beside the well and hid in it. When the serpent emerged for the sacrifice he leaped out and cut off its head. Before it died, though, the creature cursed the city, vowing that for seven years it would experience famine and drought. Hearing the threat, the people turned on the couple, who fled to the house of the girl's mother. When their pursuers arrived and told her of the serpent's curse, she instructed them to move with all their dependents to her own village, where they would have all the food and water they needed. And so the citizens took their leave of the doomed city, and Wagadu vanished once again.

The Lion of Manding

Many legends grew up about Sunjata, the founder of the empire of Mali. Even before his birth his powers were extraordinary, and as a child he was a prodigy of strength and precocious energy.

By the mid-twelfth century the empire of Ghana had collapsed, but the vacuum it left behind was soon filled by the rise of a new power, the kingdom of Mali, established by Sunjata. Few hard facts about the founder have survived, but in the folk memory he was transformed into a legendary being of more-than-mortal powers. In particular, tales of his childhood painted him as a budding Hercules, equipped with

This wooden Bambara maternity figure or *gwandusu* from Mali represents an ideal of female beauty and character. Kept in the shrine of the women's Gwan Society, it was ceremonially washed, oiled, and dressed annually.

extraordinary occult power at a time when most infants were still in the cradle.

Even before that, he gave his mother, Sugulun Konte, a hard time in the womb, forcing her to endure a pregnancy eight years long. Eventually his father—Fata Magan Cenyi, the ruler of Manding—went to a powerful *djinn* for advice. The spirit told him that the baby was in fact leaving the womb each night, but returning before dawn. To catch him, the spirit suggested leaving a mortar in the mother's bed in the hope that the baby might mistake it for home. The trick worked, and the happy news was given out that a boy had been born. His parents named him Sunjata, "Our Lion."

Saman Berete, a co-wife of Fata Magan, had, however, given birth simultaneously and there was considerable confusion as to the primogeniture of the sons, with many believing Sunjata to be the second-born who had been announced first. Sunjata's subsequent precocity was enough to provoke the co-wife into a jealous act of revenge. She had been disputing Sunjata's prior claim to the throne, but now sought help from a *djinn* in order to get rid of the young prodigy and clear the way for her son, Dankaran Tuman. Lacking the power to kill Sunjata, the spirit agreed to paralyze him instead, and for seven years the boy was unable to use his legs.

One day, with Sunjata powerless to move, his mother, Sugulun, needed baobab leaves with which to flavor the special sauce to be used in his circumcision ritual. She asked the other wives for them but they mocked, cruelly suggesting that her son should get them for her instead. Seeing his mother return home in tears, Sunjata was determined to rise to his feet and proceeded to attempt it. Sugulun searched frantically for crutches, but the iron bars she passed to him broke because of his more-than-human weight. She then cut a staff of wood and, using immense strength, he forced himself upright, walked to a baobab tree, uprooted it with his bare hands, shook out the small boys picking leaves and presented it to his mother.

By no means everyone was pleased to see him back even stronger than before. No longer crippled, his revitalized claim to the throne made him a danger. Jealous of his powers, Dankaran Tuman, now become king, offered an ox as payment to twelve witches to kidnap and kill him. But Sunjata—who was immediately aware of the threat through his preternatural perspicacity—responded with greater generosity. Confronting the witches, he gave them a buffalo each, whereupon they restored to life the ox they had butchered for food and returned it to Dankaran Tuman.

But Sunjata wished to avoid sibling strife and, having become a mighty hunter, he exiled himself by leaving for the bush, where he lived by tracking down animals. In the meantime, Manding was invaded by the sorcerer-king Sumanguru and members of Sunjata's family were killed or forced to flee the oppressive regime of this man, who was said to wear clothes made of human skin.

The lion often served as a totemic emblem, signifying courage, ferocity, magical power and leadership. Djenne terracotta lion figure, 12th–15th centuries.

The women of the family missed Sunjata sorely and eventually his mother and a sister went with a party of hunters to find him. When they tracked him down, he refused to return to Manding, so they decided to stay with him. After seven years, however, the clamor for help from the people chafing under the yoke of Sumanguru was too strong to be ignored, and Sunjata finally felt he should return to confront the tyrant.

But before he did so he sought confirmation that he was acting correctly. Thus Sunjata prayed for a sign, declaring that if he were to return his now-ill mother should die—for this would signal the total transfer of her power to him and validate his right to reign. That night Sugulun passed away.

Sunjata approached the local king for a plot in which to bury his mother. The king wanted gold, but Sunjata offered only arrowheads, pot shards, dust, and bird feathers. This "riddle" was interpreted for the ruler as meaning Sunjata would make war on him, break his town like an old pot, reduce the houses to dust, and birds would play in the ruins. Payment was then waived and an army was provided instead.

In the war that ensued, the sorcerer's magic proved too strong at first. But one of Sunjata's sisters offered to seduce Sumanguru and find out the secret of his power. She discovered that he could be harmed only by an arrow tipped with the spur of a white rooster.

Together they made the potent item, and prepared to use it in the next battle—but Sumanguru sensed it and fled. Sunjata's forces pursued the tyrant to a river and when he slowed to leap over it on his horse, he was shot. He, his wife, and his horse were turned to stone at Koulikoro, where they are still revered. Sunjata had become the undisputed king of the Manding.

125

The Queen of Sheba's Son

For centuries Ethiopia's kings have had their authority legitimized through the story of their descent from Solomon and the Queen of Sheba and the transfer of the Ark of the Covenant to safe-keeping in their kingdom.

Among Africa's historic kingdoms, Ethiopia was always the odd one out. Closer in many respects to the countries around the Red Sea, Ethiopia rose to prominence in ancient times as Axum, a trading partner of Saba in southern Arabia—the Biblical Sheba. The Arab connection gave it an ethnically mixed population in which Semitic and African strains blended. Culturally, the nation early developed a written alphabet, along with the Geez language, a precursor of modern Amharic still in use for religious purposes today. But the most significant division came later, with Ethiopia's conversion to Christianity in the fourth century CE. From that

time on, it formed the southernmost part of the medieval Christian world, and following the Muslim conquests of the seventh century its continuity with Egypt was broken and it survived as a Christian island in a non-Christian sea.

In time the separate ties to Saba and to the Christian faith fused in the legend of the nation's founder, Menelik I, from whom later kings traced their descent, a tale that remains important to the nation's Amharic majority to this day. The story tells how, in the distant past, the land was known as Sheba and was ruled by a fearsome serpent. The monster was so bulky that strangers mistook it

for a hill. Its appetite matched its size, and it ate up not just crops, sheep, goats, and cattle but also young virgins, and if it was not fed it thrashed its coils so much that earthquakes resulted.

For many years the snake plagued the land, until one day a stranger appeared offering to rid the country of the scourge. To do so, he required only a pure white lamb and a bowl of the poisonous sap of the euphorbia tree. Approaching the creature, he first offered up the lamb, which it ate whole. Then, to slake its thirst, it lapped up the euphorbia juice, and was soon convulsed in its death throes. The local people were so grateful that they asked the man to stay on as their ruler.

He governed wisely for many years until his death, when power passed to his daughter Makeda, the famous Queen of Sheba. Her realm prospered as a center of trade, and it was from merchants that she first heard of Solomon, the powerful monarch whose capital was Jerusalem. The more she learned of his wealth and wisdom,

In Ethiopia the cross has served as an important religious and protective symbol, in numerous forms, since the 4th century when Christianity was first adopted. Processional Cross, pre-19th century.

the keener she became to see the splendors of his kingdom for herself.

Eventually she decided to act on her wishes. She loaded a caravan of camels with gold and silver, precious cloths, rare perfumes, and all the other wonders that her kingdom could provide. Then she set out on the long trek north to Jerusalem, where she was welcomed by Solomon, who was much impressed not just by the gifts she brought but also by her own youth and beauty.

The king insisted that she and her entourage should stay as guests in the royal palace. Makeda was at first perturbed to find beds made up for herself and her chief lady-in-waiting in Solomon's own sleeping quarters, separated from the royal couch only by a curtain; but she was mollified by his assurance that court etiquette required no less. She was as struck by Solomon's charismatic presence as he was with her.

When the time came for the royal party to return to Sheba, not just Makeda but also her lady-in-waiting were pregnant. Before they departed, Solomon gave each of them a gold ring to pass on to their future offspring.

Both women later bore sons. Makeda named hers Menelik, and he grew up to be a handsome and intelligent young man. The queen made no secret of her intention to make him her heir, but her subjects jibbed at the idea of being ruled by a man with no known father. Their qualms reached the ears of Menelik himself, who went to his mother and insisted on learning the truth of his paternity. Only then did Makeda reveal to him that

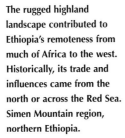

The rugged highland landscape contributed to Ethiopia's remoteness from much of Africa to the west. Historically, its trade and influences came from the north or across the Red Sea. Simen Mountain region, northern Ethiopia.

127

he was the son of the famous Solomon. Menelik at once determined to go to the king and seek his acknowledgment. Makeda raised no objections, seeing Solomon's approval as a necessary prerequisite if the youth was to succeed to the throne.

When news of the planned trip reached the lady-in-waiting, she also decided to send her son, for a plot was taking shape in her mind. Realizing that Solomon would not know who was who, she thought that if hers could reach Jerusalem first he could pass himself off as the future heir of Sheba.

But the lad had little of his father's wisdom. So, when he stopped on the way to consult an old woman with oracular powers, he paid little attention to her warning. What she said was, "At your destination, what seems high will be low and low high; the leader trails behind and the follower goes in front." His heedlessness would cost him dearly.

For, when he finally arrived at the court in Jerusalem, his long-lost father was skeptical of his claims. To test the youth's mettle, the ruler decided to swap places with a courtier, reasoning that if the boy was truly a son of his he would sense the imposture. But the Sheban, unmindful of the wise woman's words, fell into the trap and did reverence to the throned impostor, calling him "Father." Displeased, Solomon sent the claimant away.

Not long after, Menelik arrived. Bemused to hear that yet another supposed relation had turned up, Solomon decided to repeat the test—only this time he dressed himself in rags and went out to the stables. But Menelik, who had also consulted the oracle, was instinctively suspicious of the robed figure he saw sitting in state, seeing nothing of his own features in the man's face. Pulling away from him, he went from courtier to courtier but found none with his likeness. Leaving the palace, he wandered in the grounds until at last he found what he was looking for in the shape of the groom tending the horses. To Solomon's amazement, the stranger flung himself at his feet, calling him "King" and "Father."

Solomon was sufficiently impressed to take him at his word, particularly when he saw the ring that he had given Makeda so long ago. He welcomed Menelik to court, and was soon treating

The Hairy Hoof

Some traditions insist that the beautiful Queen of Sheba had an unfortunate blemish—a donkey's hoof.

One Ethiopian version of the story maintains that the future queen was destined to be sacrificed to the serpent her father killed, and that when he dispatched it a drop of its blood fell on her foot, which instantly turned into a hoof. It was to rid herself of this flaw that she went to visit King Solomon, who could reputedly cure all ills.

This tradition almost certainly reflects Islamic tales to the effect that demons, fearing Solomon might marry Makeda, whispered to him that she had hairy legs and donkey's hooves. To check the truth of the story he had a glass floor built before his throne. This revealed that, although the Queen had no hooves, her legs were indeed hirsute. To solve the problem, the king ordered the spirits to create a depilatory that left his royal visitor's limbs as smooth as satin.

Popular Ethiopian art form showing Solomon and Sheba, parents of Menelik, who is depicted carrying the Ark of the Covenant.

him as his right-hand man, even seeking his opinion on the judgments for which he was famous.

Eventually the people grew discontented with the foreigner's exalted status. Solomon realized the young man had to go. Menelik consented, on one condition; since Solomon was being asked to send away his son, he insisted, his critics should do no less. So the ruler ordered every family to send its first-born with Menelik to provide him with the army he needed to establish himself in Sheba.

Solomon lavished gifts on his favorite, but the one thing Menelik really wanted he was in no position to give. This was the Ark of the Covenant, containing the stone tablets given to Moses on Mount Sinai and now kept in the Holy of Holies of Jerusalem's great Temple. And so Menelik decided to steal it. To do so, he had a copy of the Ark prepared. The night before his departure, he went to the Temple and substituted this for the real thing.

Days after he had set out for Axum with a huge host of soldiers, Jerusalem was racked by a fearsome, portentous storm. That night Solomon dreamed that a calamity had befallen the Ark, and on waking sent servants to check that it was safe. They came back with the terrible news that it had been taken. Realizing that only Menelik could be responsible, Solomon set out in pursuit.

Upon reaching Gaza Solomon received news that convinced him to turn back to Jerusalem. Buoyed by their booty's sanctity, he was told, Menelik's host was literally marching on air. The floating soldiers were led on to Axum by the Ark in a wagon that was haloed by a blinding light.

So Solomon returned home, while Menelik arrived to a hero's welcome. The sight of the Ark and of the immense host accompanying the prince convinced the people that he should be their king. Makeda had him crowned, and the dynasty he created ruled the nation for centuries, taking care to maintain a tradition of truly Solomonic justice.

129

The Wise and Peaceful King

Many African peoples look back to golden ages under just and far-sighted rulers, but for the Bushoong of southeastern Congo, Shamba Bolongongo was the greatest king of all. During his reign his people prospered, benefiting from his wisdom and justice.

According to tradition, Shamba was a real-life ruler, said to be the ninety-third of his line. He probably reigned in the early seventeenth century, when the peoples on the southern fringes of the equatorial rainforest were coming together into large political federations. For the Bushoong of later times he was not just the model of a good ruler but also a culture hero, credited with the introduction of many essential features of their lifestyle. Above all he brought peace where previously there had been conflict and killing.

From an early age Shamba was curious to learn about the world, and as heir to the throne he insisted on traveling abroad to study the ways of other peoples. Despite his mother's warnings of the dangers of going off on his own, he spent several years away satisfying his immense natural curiosity.

And when he finally came back home, he brought with him many useful innovations he had found on his travels that he thought would be of benefit to his subjects.

So he was the first to introduce weaving and textile manufacture to the Bushongo. In particular, he showed them how to make clothing from fiber obtained from the stalks of raffia leaves in place of the rough bark they had previously used. To this day, Bushongo raffiawork is prized for its fine pile and beautiful embroidery.

He brought tobacco to the country, and the cassava plant which, along with millet, maize, and

One of Shamba's many gifts to his people was the weaving of raffiawork. Decorative raffia cloth from Congo.

The Game of *Mankala*

beans, is now a staple of the Bushoong diet. Also, he showed people how to cook the root, which can contain lethal quantities of acid, so as to remove its bitterness and dispel the poison. And he planted the first oil palms, trees that still bear the name "shamba" in the region to this day.

Yet Shamba is remembered as fondly for the things he did away with as for his importations. He forbade the use of bows and arrows in warfare, and banished the deadly four-bladed throwing knife known as the *shongo*. He hated violence, but was prepared to use whatever force was needed to keep the peace, and criminals and aggressors quickly learned to fear him. Even so, he rarely had them killed unless they refused to submit, and he invariably spared women and children, for he respected human life too much to take it unnecessarily.

His wisdom and justice were legendary, and these characteristics are emphasized in a famous wood carving that is thought to be the first portrait of any ruler of the Kuba people, of whom the Bushoong form a part. In this respect too he was a pioneer, for it became a tradition for all subsequent rulers to be portrayed as he was, squatting cross-legged with one hand grasping the dagger that symbolized kingly office.

According to the stories, one of Shamba's most successful innovations was the still-popular board game of lele or mankala.

Finding his people addicted to gambling, the king sought an alternative pastime that would occupy them in a less harmful manner. He found it in the game of *lele*, better known in the West as *mankala*, which had originally been devised in the Arab lands.

The game, which is still popular today, is played on a wooden board with up to thirty-two depressions. A number of nuts or pebbles are placed in each of the holes. Players take turns to move the counters, with the aim of ending up at a hole containing just one or two, which they can then remove and claim as their own. The player who ends up with the most counters is the winner.

Mankala **is a calculative strategy board game, thought to be the oldest in the world. Kuba-Bushoong wooden figure of Shamba, wearing his royal** *shody* **hat, playing the game.**

131

A Hero Betrayed

The Swahili of the east coast tell tales of Liongo, a tragic hero who was as famous for his poetry as for his phenomenal strength.

Liongo was very different from other African heroes. He may well have been a real-life figure; there are still people who claim descent from him today. Yet he was not a great ruler like Shamba; much of his life was spent as a fugitive. He had great strength and was a master bowman, yet he was also a poet whose songs are still remembered by ordinary Kenyans. And for all his great deeds, he died an outlaw, betrayed by his own son.

Accounts of his early life vary. He was apparently of royal blood, but not the direct heir to the throne of his kingdom, which is sometimes said to be the island of Pate, off the Kenyan coast, and by other sources to be the mainland principality of Shaka. One account makes him the eldest son of the ruler, but by a lesser wife; in the succession to the throne he therefore came behind a younger half-brother born to the sultan's principal consort.

All sources agree, though, on his immense size, strength, and courage, and on his gifts as an archer and a poet. He could cover a four-day journey on foot in a single day, and could split ivory trumpets simply by blowing through them.

It may have been his extraordinary abilities that attracted the jealousy of his half-brother. What is sure is that the ruler sought to have him killed. Fleeing the city, Liongo took refuge with the forest people, but they were bribed to bring him back dead or alive. Deciding the first option would be the easier, they cast around for a way of killing him when he would not be able to fight back. Eventually they decided to challenge him to a contest to see who could fetch the most fruit from a lofty palm tree. Their intention was to shoot him down with arrows when he was halfway up.

But Liongo suspected something was wrong. When his turn came, he took his bow and simply shot the fruit down. At that, his hosts gave up, and he was captured eventually only on a visit to Shaka to see his mother.

He was cast into the sultan's prison with his feet chained around a post and his wrists fettered. Each day his mother sent him food, but the best of it was taken by his guards and he was left with scraps. Then, after a time, word came that the sultan had decreed he must die.

He was given a final request, and asked for a *gungu* dance—a noisy communal celebration ever since associated with his name—to be performed outside his cell. Meanwhile, he taught the slave-girl who brought him his food the words of a new

The delicate sands and beautiful palms of the Zanzibar coast are said to be Liongo's traditional homeland, although the nearby Kenyan island of Pate is also cited.

poem—one instructing his mother to bake a cake of chaff and bran with a file in it. She understood at once, preparing not just the bran cake but also a spiced one made with the finest flour. Needless to say, the guards took the treat, passing on to Liongo the untempting fodder he wanted.

The poet used the noise of the dancers to cover the sound of filing. Then, free at last, he burst through the prison door. Seizing his two guards by the neck, he banged their heads together, killing them both. Then he broke out of the gaol and took to the woods as a fugitive.

For months he lived as an outlaw, raiding villages and plundering travelers. Many times the sultan sent soldiers to seize him, but every attempt failed. It seemed he could not be killed by sword or spear or any normal weapon.

Finally, at his wits' end, the ruler decided that his last hope lay in treachery. By threats, bribes, and promises he cajoled Liongo's own son into going to his father to worm out the secret of his invulnerability.

By that time Liongo seems to have become tired of life, for even though he quickly realized that the young man had come to betray him he did not send him away. Instead he willingly revealed his fatal secret—that the only weapon that could kill him was a copper needle driven into his navel.

The son returned with the news, and a suitable tool was quickly prepared. Then he went back to his father. Finding him asleep after a hard morning's hunting, he drove in the nail and fled as fast as his feet could carry him.

Liongo woke in agony. Knowing that he was dying, he snatched up his bow and arrows and strode toward the town. He reached a spot midway between the gates and the well where the citizens went to fetch water, then could go no farther. Sinking to his knees, he drew his bow for a last time—and then died.

But he did not fall. Rigor mortis set in quickly, freezing his body in a shooting posture. Looking out from the city walls, the inhabitants saw him apparently guarding the path to the well and did not dare venture out of the gates. For three days the city went without fresh water. Eventually the elders persuaded the hero's mother to go and plead with him, and so it was she who first discovered that her son was dead.

A threat no longer, he was given a burial fitting his rank, and a mound said to be his grave still remains near Kipini. But his real monuments were his poems, which are not only read by scholars but remain on the lips of ordinary Swahili to this day.

Horns of carved elephant tusk were used in African royal courts as instruments and were blown during battle or bestowed ritually as grave goods. It was believed that their notes could be understood by the dead. Liongo was said to be so strong he could split such ivory trumpets merely by blowing into them. Ivory horn decorated with humans, deer, and reptiles.

THE AFRICAN LEGACY

The cultural traditions of Africa stretch way beyond its borders, for the forced migrations of the Atlantic slave trade took place on a vast scale: historians estimate that at its peak in the 1780s about 78,000 slaves each year made the arduous journey to the Americas against their will—perhaps 14 million people over the entire three-century period.

Most New World transportees came from West Africa, but many hailed from other parts including some from the east. Tribal traditions were diverse, and while in some places individual cultures survived, in most they mingled with one another and European influences to create a rich, new blend.

A carnival headdress from Trinidad. Calypso music, which dominates the Caribbean festival, is derived from African musical forms.

Trickster Folktales

African folktales and legends were transplanted into new soil. The Ananse stories of the Akan lived on in the West Indies and the southern states of the United States. In Jamaica—where the spider's exploits were told at funerals and wakes—he even kept his old name. In South Carolina and Georgia, the trickster changed genders and became Miss or Aunt Nancy. Today, the era of multicultural education has enabled the crafty spider to gain new audiences for his exploits.

Also in the southern United States the Bantu trickster hare was transformed into Brer Rabbit, a familiar figure to generations of children through the books of the white American journalist Joel Chandler Harris (1848–1908). Beginning with *Tales of the Old Plantation* (1881), Harris produced a series of ten books in which an old black servant named Uncle Remus recounted animal stories of the African-American South—starring Brer Rabbit but also featuring Brer Bear and Brer Wolf; brer was "brother" in the dialect used by Uncle Remus.

Africa's Musical Legacy

During the long Atlantic crossing into slavery, captive Africans were permitted—sometimes forced—to dance and sing. After arriving in the New World they were usually allowed to keep their musical traditions alive, although drums were sometimes banned. The plantation owners appear to have seen music as a way of dissipating anger and averting violence.

Plantation slaves sang as they labored under the punishing sun. An individual would sing a line and his workmates would provide the response in a leader-chorus form derived from an African model; the same rhythmic pattern was found in the "spirituals" sung at times of worship.

Various, distinctive African-American forms of folk music developed in the American South, but among the best known were those born at the turn of the century from the interactions of African-derived elements with European traditions: jazz and the blues. Jazz emerged in New Orleans in the music of the parade bands and in the small bars of the city's Storyville area where great artists such as Louis Armstrong (1901–1971) and Sidney Bechet (1897–1959) played. Musical historians trace a direct correspondence between the syncopations of jazz and the counter-rhythms of traditional West African instrumental music.

The first blues emerged a little earlier than jazz, sung by black songsters at traveling "medicine shows." The first written blues came in 1909 with "Mr Crump Blues" credited to W.C. Handy (1873–1958) of Memphis, Tennessee. The blues' African links are strong. In its developed form the blues song—a crooning lament about hardship, loss, or cruel treatment at the hands of a lover—can be traced clearly to an African genre, the song of complaint, gossip, and news (also reflected later in West Indian calypso). The tradition of the griot in West Africa—a bard and storyteller preserving tribal memory in song—also influenced the blues.

Both jazz and blues have had enduring lives as separate musical forms and have also fed into the explosion of musical styles that has characterized the twentieth century. Popular music in its present form would be unimaginable without them.

Survival of the African Gods
Most plantation masters promoted Christianity and would not allow slaves to practice African religious rituals. But many slaves refused to abandon their ancestors' traditions: a few met clandestinely; many converted but continued to follow African religion, creating a hybrid faith with elements of both. Three religions practiced today in South America and the Caribbean reflect this mix.

A taste for "World Music" has brought African rhythms in all their great variety to a widespread audience. Baaba Maal is only one of many musicians and singers today with a global audience.

In the Brazilian religion of Macumba, Yoruba gods are associated with Christian saints. One strand, Candomble, thrives in the region around the port city of Bahia in northeastern Brazil. Rituals include animal sacrifices and dances led by drums while also making use of the cross and intercessions to the saints. Devotees associate Ogun, Yoruba *orisha* of iron and war, with Saint George, and Sango, *orisha* of the thunderbolt, with Saint Jerome. Yemoja—a wife of Ogun and a river goddess—is celebrated as Iemanja, a sea deity, and identified with the Virgin Mary. Another strand, Umbanda, is particularly popular in Rio de Janeiro and Sao Paolo, having a more spiritualist slant and drawing elements from Buddhism and Hinduism.

The African-Brazilian religions are no minority cult: devotees include many practicing Catholics and people from all classes and races. Offerings to

135

the sea and to Iemanja are part of traditional New Year celebrations in Rio de Janeiro and in a Bahia festival on February 2. Recent figures indicate 30 million followers in Brazil alone.

In Cuba and parts of the United States, Santeria also associates Yoruba gods with Christian saints. Its followers recognize a supreme god called Olorun or Olodumare, and identify him with God the Father of Christianity. Spirits or *orishas* control life on Earth and devotees offer animal sacrifices and prayers to them to win their support.

Probably the best known of these African-derived religions, however, is Haiti's *vodoun* or voodoo. Some of Haiti's slaves were from West African Fon and Yoruba territories, while others came from the Congo region. The name *vodoun* derives from the Fon word for a god, *vodun*, but the name for gods or spirits in *vodoun* itself is the Congo word *loa*. The *loa* are thought to be willing to act as individual and family protectors in return for ritual service and worship. *Vodoun* religious services are led by priests or *houngan*—a Fon word, meaning "spirit chief"—and priestesses or *mambo*. Features include African-derived dance, drumming, and animal sacrifice. Many followers also attend the Roman Catholic Church.

The rites of this folk religion have been sensationalized in many a film, with particular reference to the *Vodoun* concept of the zombie: a dead person's soul or a corpse raised from the grave and given the power to walk and talk. *Houngans* are sometimes said to use a poison that turns the living into zombies. The earlier zombie films were set on Caribbean islands and the zombie picture became a subgenre of the horror film.

Jamaican Rastafarianism is distinct from all these religions in that it neither derives from African tradition nor incorporates Christian elements. But it does look to Africa as the homeland of the black race. Followers believe that Ethiopia's Emperor Haile Selassie (1892–1975)—descended from Solomon and also named Ras Tafari—was the incarnation of the immortal God and has lived on in his people since his corporeal death. Their name for God is Jah and they believe that they live in

Traditional chieftainship survives in many parts of Africa, although the power of the incumbent is often circumscribed by the influence of religious elders. *Oba* Akenzua II in his ceremonial regalia, Benin City, Nigeria, 1964.

exile from their earthly Ethiopian paradise under a system dominated by white people. Much of their imagery became familiar through the work of the reggae musician Bob Marley (1945–1981).

The Traditional in New Forms

The countries of Africa have gone through rapid change and frequent conflict in the twentieth century, but many old ways continue to be honored. One example is West Africa's enduring oral tradition. Professional griots, for instance, survived in the 1990s: some performed on the radio and many issued recordings. In addition amateur storytellers still travel the region putting on performances of tales. Told at night in a communal setting, the events begin with riddles, then proceed to the tale, with the use of many voices and perhaps even makeup to indicate different characters. Songs and question-and-answer repartee with the audience are integral parts of the entertainment.

Senegalese filmmaker Ousmane Sembene (1923–2007) once said that he sees himself and filmmakers generally as working in the same domain as the griots and storytellers—and in some sense as their heirs. African cinema only came to life in the early 1960s. Previously, African people could learn technical skills in the Colonial Film Units (CFUs), but the units did not encourage Africans to make films in line with their own traditions.

In the post-colonial era many African filmmakers focussed on folkloric elements in their work. Sembene's 1966 film *La Noirede* (*Black Girl*)—sub-Saharan Africa's first feature-length picture—told the tragic tale of a African servant girl taken to France by her employers. There she feels isolated and finally commits suicide; the African -mask that she has brought with her to Europe becomes a symbol of West African culture in its clash with a dominant Europe. More recently *Keita! L'Heritage du Griot* (*Keita! The Voice of the Griot*; 1994), directed by Dani Kouyate from Burkina Faso, recounted the tale of a boy who learns the mythology of his people from a griot. *Taafe Fanga* (*Skirt Power*, 1997), directed by Adama Drabo of Mali, dramatized a myth of the local Dogon people: when the women come into possession of a ritually powerful mask they use it to force their menfolk to swap roles with them—while the men perform domestic tasks the women enjoy the hunt and take power.

African cinema has won many plaudits in the 1980s and 1990s, taking awards at several international film festivals. At the same time African music is popular, writers have won enthusiastic acclaim (a Nobel Prize for Literature for Wole Soyinka in 1986, for example) and African art forms are admired worldwide. In many ways—both in Africa itself and by dissemination through the countries in the Americas that were the new home of the first slaves—the continent's traditional culture has had a remarkably enduring legacy. Through folklore, cultural attitudes, religion, and particularly music Africa has left a deep and immeasurably enriching mark on the world.

Cinema in Francophone West Africa has far outstripped that in English-speaking Africa with the help of funding from France. This scene is from *Sarraounia*, a 1986 film from Burkina Faso, directed by Med Hondo.

137

Glossary

abiku Soul of a Yoruba who died in child-hood but keeps returning by being born time and again to the same parents.

akachekulu Bush spirits who granted the Bantu people the right to settle in their land.

akuaba Akan doll, meaning "Akua's child," named after a childless woman who became pregnant after commissioning such a figure.

a-mantsho-nga-tshol Serpent spirit among the Baga, often shown in a stylized carving.

babalaawo Initiates in the *ifa* divination system of the Yoruba.

biloko Evil, sharp-toothed, human-eating, dwarves living in Central Africa's forests.

Fa The god of *ifa* divination, as practiced among the Fon of the Dahomey kingdom.

houngan Priest or "spirit chief" in the *vodoun* religion.

ibeji The name given to twins among the Yoruba. They had their own protective deity called Ibeji who punished families that failed to treat the two children kindly.

ifa "All-embracing," the divination system devised by the Yoruba and presided over by the god Orunmila; also practiced by the Fon.

kabaka The king of the Buganda people of East Africa (modern-day Uganda).

kanga Baule scarification lines around the mouth of both sexes, intended to guard against disease and bad luck.

kisirani People in East Africa unwittingly possessed by an evil power that causes harm and misery all around them.

li Ngbandi word for cannibal spirits that enter the stomach and possess people.

lisaje "Lisa's beads," meaning those belonging to Mawu-Lisa, the androgynous creator figure of the Fon and left on Earth by a couple who came down from the sky.

loa Gods or spirits in the *vodoun* religion.

mfecane The territorial expansion of the Zulu and the death and displacement of southern African peoples—the "crushing"—during the early nineteenth century.

moshambwooy A spirit mask from the Kuba-speaking Bushoong of Congo. It represents their founder figure, Woot.

mukenge Bushoong-influenced type of mask found among the Ngeende of Congo, recognized by its stylized elephant trunk. Sometimes also called *mukyeem*.

nduen fobara Carved memorial screen forming part of a family shrine among the Kalabari people of Nigeria.

ngesh Water spirits from whom Bushoong diviners derive their supernatural powers.

ngulu A Kota reliquary figure placed to watch over the bones of an ancestor.

nkondi A type of *nkisi* or empowered statue of the Kongo people, distinctive due to its protruding nails.

oba Ruler of a Nigerian kingdom or city.

odun egungun "Festivals for the ancestors" held by the Yoruba.

orisha Lesser deity of Yoruba religion who people looked to for protection.

umkovu Zulu zombie incapable of speech because of a slit tongue.

vodun A lesser god of Fon religion; *vodoun* or *voodoo* derives from the word.

yetenkonde Bush spirits who granted the Somba the right to settle in their land.

zimbabwe A Shona word whose various meanings include "house of stone" and "sacred structure."

For More Information

African American Museum
Fair Park
3536 Grand Avenue
Dallas, TX 75210-1005
(214) 565-9026
Web site: http://www.aamdallas.org
Museum dedicated to the research, identification, selection, acquisition, presentation, and preservation of visual art forms and historical documents that relate to the African American community.

The DuSable Museum of African American History
740 East 56th Place
Chicago, IL 60637
Web site: http://www.dusablemuseum.org
Museum dedicated to collecting, preserving, and displaying artifacts and objects that promote understanding and inspire appreciation of the achievements, contributions, and experiences of African Americans through exhibits, programs, and activities that illustrate African American history, culture, and art.

Museum for African Art
36-01 43rd Avenue
Long Island City, NY 11101
(718) 784-7700
Web site: http://www.africanart.org
Museum dedicated to increasing public understanding and appreciation of African art and culture.

Museum of African American History
14 Beacon Street, Suite 719
Boston, MA 02108
(617) 725-0022
Web site: http://www.afroammuseum.org
New England's largest museum dedicated to preserving, conserving, and interpreting the contributions of African Americans.

National Museum of African American History and Culture
Capital Gallery
600 Maryland Avenue SW
Suite 7001
Washington, DC 20013
(202) 633-7369
Web site: http://nmaahc.si.edu
Museum that showcases important artifacts of African American history and culture.

Web Sites

Due to the changing nature of Internet links, Rosen Publishing has developed an online list of Web sites related to the subject of this book. This site is updated regularly. Please use this link to access the list:

http://www.rosenlinks.com/wmyth/afro

For Further Reading

Asante, Molefi Kete (ed.). *Encyclopedia of African Religion*. Sage Publications: California, 2008.

Asante, Molefi Kete. *Spearmasters: Introduction to African Religion*. University of America Press: Lanham, Maryland, 2007.

Bacquart, Jean-Baptiste. *The Tribal Arts of Africa*. Thames and Hudson: London, 1998.

Belcher, Stephen Paterson. *African Myths of Origin*. Penguin Classics: London, 2006.

Courlander, Harold. *Gods and Heroes from Yoruba Mythology*. Crown Books: New York, 1973.

Courlander, Harold. *A Treasury of African Folklore*. Marlowe & Company: New York, 1996.

Davidson, Basil. *The Story of Africa*. London, 1984.

Evans-Pritchard, E.E. *The Zande Trickster*. Clarendon Press: Oxford, 1967.

Frobenius, Leo. *The Voice of Africa. Vol. II*. Hutchinson: London, 1913.

Griaule, M. *Conversations with Ogotemmeli*. Oxford University Press: Oxford, 1956.

Herskovits, Melville and Francis. *Dahomean Narrative*. Northwestern University Press: Evanston, 1958.

Lugira, Aloysius Muzzanganda. *African Traditional Religion*. Chelsea House Publishers: New York, 2009.

McIntosh, Roderick J. *"Riddle of Great Zimbabwe"* in *Archaelogy*. July/August, 1998.

Murray, Jocelyn (ed.). *Cultural Atlas of Africa*. Checkmark Books: New York, 1998.

Niane, D.T. *Sundiata: An Epic of Old Mali*. Longman: London, 1986.

Owusu, Heike. *African Symbols*. Sterling Publishing: New York, 2007.

Parrinder, Geoffrey. *African Mythology*. Hamlyn: London, 1982.

Preston Blier, Suzanne. *Royal Arts of Africa*. Laurence King Publishing: London, 1998.

Radin, Paul (ed.). *African Folktales*. Schocken Books: New York, 1983.

Schmalenbach, W (ed.). *African Art*. Prestel-Verlag: Munich, 1988.

Visona, Monica. *A History of Art in Africa*. Prentice Hall: New Jersey, 2007.

Werner, Alice. *Myths and Legends of the Bantu*. Harrap: London, 1933.

Willett, Frank. *African Art*. Thames and Hudson: London, 1971.

Index

Page numbers in *italic* denote captions. Where there is a textual reference to the topic on the same page as a caption, italics have not been used.